CareGivers **Scare**Takers

JACKLYN RYAN

Copyright © AD 2021 Jacklyn Perry Ryan

CareGivers ScareTakers: Exposing Fraud in Senior Care

All rights reserved. Each author in this book retains the copyright to their individual section. Their submissions are printed herein with their permission. Each author is responsible for their individual opinions expressed through their words. This book reflects the author's present recollections of experiences over time. Names have been changed and events have been compressed. No part of this publication may be reproduced, distributed, or transmitted to any form or by any means, including photocopying, recording, or other electronic mechanical methods, except for brief quotations in critical reviews or articles without the prior written permission of the author.

Published by Five Vines Press: fivevinespress@gmail.com
Website: CareGiverScareTakers.com
info@caregiverscaretakers.com

Print Book ISBN : 978-1-7372807-0-5

Ebook ISBN : 978-1-7372807-1-2

TABLE OF CONTENTS

How Big is This Business?	i
About the Author	iii
Introduction	v
Forward	ix
Chapter 1: Dad's Story	1
Chapter 2: Mom's Story	39
Chapter 3: Stubborn Behavior Outweighs Logic	45
Chapter 4: Hoochie Mamma	49
Chapter 5: Who Can You Trust?	51
Chapter 6: The Useless Caregiver	57
Chapter 7: Friend or Foe	61
Chapter 8: Care From Afar	65
Chapter 9: The Trusted Caregiver	67
Chapter 10: DHS Removed Her	71
Chapter 11: Relative Rip-Off	85
Chapter 12: Crisis Related Event Lead to Losses	89
Chapter 13: The Doctor Intercedes	95
Chapter 14: They're Only as Good as the Company They Work For	101
Chapter 15: My Parents Did It Right	107
Chapter 16: NewsFlashes	111
Tips on Hiring and Brief Questionnaire	117
Brief Estate Planning and Other Key Questions	121
Resources	125

To Cayla ~
Thank you for
caring & making a difference
You know ~ are
there stories
"Only a Glimpse"
Jacklyn Ryan
Jacee

3/23

How BIG is This Business?

With an aging population, more families are struggling with dependable, trusted care. This process is riddled with problems. Our social care system is monetized from the cradle to the grave.

Let's present some statistics:

According to the Caregiving in the US 2020 report published by the National Alliance for Caregiving and AARP, 53 million Americans are providing unpaid care for relatives and friends. Most of those caregivers (41.8 million) are looking after care recipients who are age 50 or older.

According to the employment projections of the US Bureau of Labor Statistics, during 2014 – 2024, home healthcare occupations ranked among the top 10 in the list. Also, the demand for home health aides is estimated to be 2.9 million between 2016 - 2026. Hence, home healthcare providers need to find 2.9 million heads to keep up with the rising demand. (Source: US Bureau of Labor Statistics).

Currently, over 1.4M persons are employed in home health care services.

Overall, US home health spending officially hit $102.2 billion in 2018, and then soared to $113 billion in 2019, according to a new analysis from the Centers for Medicare & Medicaid Services (CMS) Office of the Actuary. The 2018 number is a more than 30% increase compared to all home health spending just five years ago.

There are 429,045 Home Care Provider businesses as of early 2021, an increase of 3.7% from 2020.

This business will continue to grow. Robots will not be replacing human care. Better regulations must be in place.

About the Author

Jacklyn Perry Ryan, CCIM, a successful Realtor who specializes in commercial real estate, has faced that heart-wrenching time in her life when her parents were no longer able to care for themselves. She is like you, a professional that was thrown into the worm hole of senior health care without knowledge. She cared for her dad over five years and her mom under hospice care for six months. She has been involved with other families and their senior care.

Contacting established home health care agencies, she discovered that appearances can be deceiving. In the trenches of caregiver nightmares, Jacklyn has learned the pitfalls and landmines of inappropriate and unscrupulous "ScareTakers." With her's and other's powerful personal stories, and extensive research on this undeniable problem, Jacklyn is armed with life-changing information that can revise the process for those looking for appropriate and trustworthy care for their loved ones.

Jacklyn is a sought-after speaker, consultant, and workshop presenter. She is available to speak for Senior centers, professional/civic organizations, attorneys/estate and financial planners.

She is a *USA Today* and *Wall Street Journal* bestselling author featured in the anthology *Success Mindsets: How Top Entrepreneurs Succeed in Business and Life* from Leaders Press.

www.CareGiverScareTakers.com
info@caregiverscaretakers.com

INTRODUCTION

Exposing Fraud and Manipulation by Caregivers and Others

"I'm standing right here to help you!"
"Ah, OK," said the client.
"You forget that part, *you need me*," the ScareTaker said.
"Every single day, I need you," the client responded.

Manipulation is rampant! More than forty million Americans are providing some type of care for an older relative. Even if your relatives are currently in sound physical and mental health, at some point they're likely to need assistance. You must understand what caregiving entails, from hiring and working with caregivers, to finding people on your own or working within an agency, to managing paperwork for insurance or medical care. At what point do you determine that your loved one needs assistance?

The crux of the problem? Vulnerability. When we are children, we rely on our parents. When we are in our elder years, who can we depend upon? Who can we trust? Can we trust our adult children to make proper decisions for our care? Sometimes the roles must reverse. There is a song written by Wood Newton, "Daddy went to Heaven in a Pickup Truck." In it is a verse that says, "Once a man, twice a child."

What can be done? Ideally, you want to have a frank discussion with your family while minds are still clear. All should be present, even if virtually. If you don't have a sibling, enlist a mutual friend or someone familiar with your family when you have the conversation. This person will serve as a comfort for both of you, and, as a witness.

Some adult children and seniors find it very difficult to discuss the "golden years." Now, some are calling it the "rusty years" because those golden years are not perceived as golden as they once were. This book's stories illustrate different situations that have arisen because of a lack of communication, misunderstandings, fraudulent caregivers, and other opportunists.

Some of us "adult children" are self-sufficient and do not need our parents' money. We love our parents, with or without their money. It doesn't matter. We want them to have the best care. However, we cannot always fulfill our parents' want to be needed. In past days, our family generations were more connected and cohesive. The grandparents had a sense of purpose to care for their kids and grandkids. Our generation has split off from that. We have families of our own, with jobs and bills to pay, just like our parents once had. If the grandparents can be involved and want to be involved, it helps the family considerably. Unfortunately, most dysfunctional families evolve to non-cohesiveness, thus the grandparents may not feel a sense of Purpose.

They are then "prime" for a manipulative caregiver to take advantage. Sadly, it takes just one unethical caregiver in a trusted position to turn the family upside down and inside out.

I wrote this book to share my and other "adult children's" personal challenges and horrific situations. This book can serve as a gateway to communication between you and your family. I want you to avoid AND overcome the difficulties that I and others have experienced. I am not alone, and neither are you. Many of us come from dysfunctional families, and it is up to us to help one another on our journey with our loved ones during their last quarter.

As you are reading about these experiences, you may say that these incidents could never happen to you. Well, I could have never imagined it!

Introduction

There's no guarantee that a caregiver will not *turn on you* or defraud you, or that you are isolated from scams. The names have been changed to protect the innocent...and the Guilty!

It doesn't matter that one is rich or poor, a farmer or city dweller, nice or not. What matters is that this generation worked hard physically and mentally, built businesses based upon handshakes, and were not accustomed to unscrupulous and manipulative people in a position of trust.

The book cover reflects the unscrupulous caregivers, who are placed in positions of trust, that may begin manipulating your heartstrings. Then, before you know it, leading them to your purse strings. It is rarely obvious, and usually subtle. The descriptive word **ScareTaker** is coined from the scary stories and the persons responsible for them. Besides, the terms "caregivers" and "caretakers" are used interchangeably.

The persons placed in your position of trust, caring for your loved ones, more than likely are paid around minimum wage. ***Raising the bar on caregiver qualifications will also raise the bar when it comes to the quality of care.***

If you have hired a wonderful and well-qualified caregiver, consider yourself lucky and blessed. But, don't let your guard down. There is a Tips on Hiring and Questionnaire at the back of this book to help you better qualify an agency or an independent caregiver.

Just because you are coherent and getting along well doesn't mean that you shouldn't be wearing a Life Alert device. What if you are living alone and have a stroke? And your phone is on the counter while you are lying on the floor?

While, for now, you seem to have everything "under control," there are frequent hospital visits, and your house is very cluttered. Who is to determine *everything is ok*?

There needs to be an open discussion of physical concerns. This should include practicalities around the home and transportation. Additionally, there should be a discussion of legal issues such as power of attorney (POA), do not resuscitate (DNR), living will, and other matters related to estate planning. Also important are discussions of financial issues. Is there a will and a trust? Is there a payable on death (POD) on the financial accounts? This is just the tip of the iceberg. Review and complete the questionnaire in the back of this book and visit with an estate attorney.

If any of these items are not addressed, someone else or the government can suddenly become involved in *your* family's affairs. This book aims to help your family begin a conversation regarding your state of affairs and potential threats. I need to emphasize—

Do not wait for a crisis to happen!

This is a collection of real-life, true anecdotes that happened but are frequently only exposed in courtrooms or behind closed doors. Hopefully, this book will raise the awareness of seniors and their adult children. It hopes to encourage these critical and essential discussions about qualified personal care of your loved ones. It will encourage you to think about where the care will be provided, and how other essential medical, financial, and legal decisions will be made. Above all, this book will make you, the responsible person, understand that someone must be an *advocate and watchdog*!

FORWARD

Dedicated to the Vulnerable Seniors and
the Adult Children—We Do our Best

"Oh, thank you for helping me. The breakfast was delicious," acknowledged the client.

"You're welcome, and I'm glad you like it! I'm sorry I was late, but I had car trouble," replied the caregiver.

The client continued, "Oh, really? What happened?"

The caregiver answered, "The old car has several problems, and I can't afford to fix it."

The rather wealthy and lonely client answered, "Well, honey, maybe I can help you with that."

Aside from outright stealing items and money from a client, the above is a possible scenario of how collaborative manipulation and fraud begins. It may seem quite innocent at first, but this small bit of *help* can and frequently does balloon into a continually codependent relationship. The client has his or her need to feel important and in control fulfilled, and the caregiver mushrooms into a *scaretaker* learning to exploit the clients' needs and generosity.

Like all professional relationships, boundaries are assumed and must be adhered to, but in close interpersonal relationships that inevitably develop in caregiving situations, it is very easy for boundaries to become blurred and then, nonexistent. So, who is at fault? The short answer is, the *caregiver*.

A family is hiring caregivers, and their integrity is the number one reason for the trust placed in them by the client's family. Many seniors, especially widowed men, are incredibly lonely and exhibit extreme neediness when it comes to displaying the former prowess and egotistical self-importance of their younger days.

Also, in many cases, the client's family may be somewhat dysfunctional, and some of the members may be at odds with both the elderly client and each other. I believe these situations are more than common, even in better functioning families. The loneliness and mental depression that often accompanies our "rusty years" contribute to our vulnerability, weakness, and susceptibility to a charming salesman, whether it be a caregiver, a roofer, a paver, or a sweepstakes promotor/fraudster.

As you read these true stories, various people in the author's situation have exploited her naive and gullible father. As she began to research her topic, many people came forward with stories of their own, some the victims of inside-the-family fraud, and others the victims of professional caregivers and scam artists.

The topic of this book is one that often-embarrassed victims are reluctant to expose and discuss. However, the problem of senior fraud and abuse is widespread and costs victims millions of dollars every year. What a tragedy to have a nest egg, the result of a life of good decisions and hard work, be compromised or even destroyed by con artists and criminals!

Particularly in the case of the author's father, you will gain insight into what happens to the minds of people as they age. The decline of their mental state is exacerbated by the loss of a spouse and the decrease in their physical viability. Many become frantically lonely, and what happens when anxiety and loneliness take over? One's good sense and decision-making capabilities seem to fly away with the wind.

The combination of investigation and legislation must be in the future of this growing and fraud-ridden problem.

Max Ryan, husband and partner in everything.

CAREGIVERS
SCARETAKERS

Chapter 1

Dad's Story

My dad, Jack, was born in 1932 to a poor farming family at the height of the Great Depression. He grew up working on the family farm, raising cattle, growing food crops, and helping with the family's poultry business.

In high school, he wanted to play football so bad, if he couldn't hitch a ride home after practices or games, he would walk the five miles, in the dark. He relayed a story that one night, he heard a panther scream. It made the hairs on the back of his neck rise! His parents never attended any practices or games.

He spent a significant amount of time on a horse, working cattle, and even did a little bull riding in the local rodeo. It was a "rough and tumble" upbringing, and Jack was no stranger to the often-mischievous acts of many teenagers.

His personality was primarily handed down on the maternal side of his family tree. Jack's mother had a reputation around town as a hard-working, hard-driving Baptist woman who might hit you with a cast-iron skillet if she took a dislike to you. Indeed, she was abusive at times. Likewise, Jack grew up being a bully. What Jack wanted; he found a way to get. He was somewhat slight in stature but scrappy.

Like most bullies, he was really looking for love and attention, a little fuel for his up-and-coming narcissistic personality.

Dad spent the first forty years or so of his life farming and ranching. He married twice in his life, and his first wife, my mom, was a well-raised and engaging young woman who likely found Dad's wooing to be exciting and his craziness stimulating. They married and lived on the farm. My brother, Ty, and I were born in 1958 and 1961, respectively, and life seemed on track. However, once we started attending school, Mom wanted to move to town. Dad continued to work the farm, but his inherent restlessness and voyeurism began to take hold as his family responsibilities grew. He began looking for more excitement and attention from other women outside his home.

He also had developed a significant drinking problem. One of my vivid memories from childhood was waking up on Christmas Eve to a noise banging in the living room. I walked into the room and saw Dad on a pogo stick drunkenly bouncing around, crashing into furniture, ending up on the floor. After many such episodes involving drinking, abuse, and infidelity, Mom divorced him, taking us with her to live in a small town nearby. She just didn't need another child to raise.

Dad found significant success in the business world by going into partnership with a neighbor, a skilled engineer, who had invented industrial machines that businesses badly needed. By that time he had met and married his second wife, June, with whom he had become acquainted while placing a newspaper ad for a farmworker.

June was a strong, very astute businesswoman who had already successfully managed the local newspaper's advertising department. She became an essential part of Dad's fledgling business by using her family inheritance, helping him buy out his partner and make the business's first big score by selling its products to an up-and-coming Fortune 500 company. Dad made other investments with his newfound financial success, most of which lost money. He was and truly is what many call a dream chaser and a rainbow seeker.

After many years, with June alongside him in the business, Dad, with her prodding, invited her son, George, to join them. Over decades,

Chapter 1: Dad's Story

the business grew and prospered to become one of the largest of its kind in the world. Amid that success, Dad sold the business to George, giving Dad significant income as he headed toward retirement and hobby farming.

~ * ~

I had been living in Texas for a couple of decades. After 9/11 happened, I began thinking of returning to my family because I was concerned about their aging and June, who had battled cancer earlier, was dealing with it again. Dad deeded me ten acres and I built my home on the hill where my great grandparents had homesteaded. My home construction was completed in 2003. I can see Dad and June's house from where I live.

Dad had always seemed to have lady luck following him around, but in 2004, one very unlucky loss happened—June died of cancer. She had spent many tumultuous years with him, helping him farm, fish, hunt, and participate in all the activities Dad held so dearly. Had she stayed on the scene, his later years would have had a good monitor and enforcer. However, life took a turn. He was left very lonely and angry, now fumbling around for himself. Soon, he met his first girlfriend, Shelly. Others didn't stay with him due to his wild drinking, late-night phone calls, impromptu 2 a.m. visits, and other erratic behavior. Shelly made the best of it and ended up taking him for around $100K to start a skincare business that never got off the ground. After a few years, Jack lost interest in her and moved on to my friend, Lisa.

Lisa and I became friends through our favorite outdoor activity, horseback riding. After a particular trail ride, the weather became threatening and I invited Lisa to stay at my house for the night. The storm came with winds forceful enough to shake the windows. Through the driving rain, I saw headlights coming up the hill. Dad knew Lisa was staying overnight, so he used the excuse to check on us and visit Lisa.

Thus began the relationship between Jack and Lisa. "Lee-sa," as she would sometimes pronounce her name, was ten years older than me. She was a somewhat whacky professor at a local junior college who enjoyed horses and being at the farm. She was indeed an interesting person and better educated than most of Dad's peers and friends, so she captured his interest. They became lovers, and, at one point, Dad was pushing her to marry him.

One summer, he persuaded her not to teach summer school, offering her $10,000 to live with him, so she accepted the money and agreed to the arrangement. She stayed only two weeks after becoming depressed by experiencing his daily heavy drinking and smoking, his abusive behavior, and uncontrollable temper. Though she could not live with him, Dad persisted in chasing after her, showering her with cash, working around her small farm, and the relationship continued. At times, she referred to him as *trash with cash*.

A few years passed, and Lisa was approaching retirement age. She was tiring of Dad and the crisis-driven lifestyle that she had with him. He had increased his drinking and was sending copious numbers of $20 bills off to sweepstakes.

One day he announced to Lisa in his yelling boastful voice, "I've won a new Mercedes Benz, and it will be here next week. All I have to do is pay the freight of $1,500!"

~ * ~

One evening, Dad called me to come to his house. He showed me an envelope from an out-of-state resident. It was an age-stained, musty-smelling envelope that contained a chain letter with an $800 check. I called the check's owner since there was a phone number on it and a senior woman named Gladys answered the phone.

She said her instructions were to mail her check to Dad, and he would add another one and send it on to the next person on the list. These instructions arrived to her via a phone call from scam artists about the day the check arrived. Each person was promised $10,000.00 within the year. I told Gladys this was a scam and that I was tearing up the check and returning the pieces to her. Then, threatening phone calls from the scammers began.

Chapter 1: Dad's Story

Soon, Dad became involved in more serious scams targeting unsuspecting elderly folks carried out by professional fraudsters from Jamaica, Canada, and Las Vegas.

"Hello, is this Jack Foster? Congratulations, my friend! You have won a million dollars in the sweepstakes you entered. Now, our code word we will be using is 'Blue Sky.' I tell you, my friend, the money is waiting for you, and we want to rush it to you. All you have to do is wire us $3,000, so we can get it through customs."

Scammers were constantly calling. Dad had gotten into a *ring*. The Jamaican scammers were amazingly persuasive and persistent. My husband, Patrick, my stepbrother, George, and I did everything we thought we could to convince Dad that these were scams and to ignore them, but to no avail. Remember, we're dealing with a rainbow seeker and a dream chaser!

One morning, I received one such call on my phone! Dad had told the scammer about his daughter who lives on the hill. The scammer asked me why I wouldn't allow Dad to get his money. I told the scammer off and hung up on him.

I was at Dad's house one morning, when he was leaving for town. I stayed there to monitor his landline phone. I was on the phone with the scammers when he returned. He showed me a bank receipt wiring $3,000 to a Jamaican bank. I rushed to the bank, attempting to reverse the transaction, but it was too late. It was already completed. The bank employee had tried to explain to Dad that this was a scam and he should not do this, but he wouldn't listen. The next morning he received another call.

"Jack, your money is here in Little Rock, but we are having a little customs problem. We need another $2,000 to get it through customs."

I took the phone away from him and demanded to speak to the customs officer.

The scammer replied, "I am the customs officer."

Have you ever spoken to a customs officer in Little Rock, Arkansas, with a Jamaican accent?

After several *go to hells* and other threatening phone calls, they finally told Dad that they knew where he lived and that they were coming to get him. They told him, "We know you live down a curvy dead-end road. You have a statue at your driveway entrance and two blue trucks."

Thanks, Google Earth!

After that phone call, he had more to drink and passed out for the night. The next morning, Patrick and I went to his house. He was sitting at the kitchen bar with a revolver on the counter and a shotgun nearby. I called the local county prosecutor's office and my state's Attorney General's office but received absolutely no help.

Another day, I noticed Dad driving up the hill toward town much faster than usual. I jumped in my car and followed him. He pulled into his bank's parking lot and went in. I walked up behind him and listened. He was ordering a $9,500 cashier's check!

I tapped him on the shoulder and said, "Whatcha doin', Dad?"

He replied, "I'm gettin' a check."

I grabbed his keys and told the teller to cancel the transaction.

On the way into town, I had called George and asked him to meet us at the bank. The two of us had a stern talk with Dad, and he agreed to stop the nonsense. Of course, that was wishful thinking. Irrational behavior was his norm. What we didn't know at the time was that he had already wired around $45,000 to various scammers. George removed his landline telephone and gave him a cell phone in case the number would need to be changed again. The calls ceased.

I also fended off road pavers and roofers. Seniors are *sitting ducks*. It's especially important to use discretion when contacted by strangers. But as some seniors age, they lose the filter of reason. There are many phone and computer scams that look and sound identical to your bank or investments—even the Social Security Administration attempting to get access to your financial accounts and passwords! Always communicate with family or friends. If someone contacts you for money, really, *Just Hang Up*!

Chapter 1: Dad's Story

~ * ~

Back to "Lee-sa." She announced to Dad that she was going to retire and move across country to an equestrian community 1,000 miles away. She was leaving her *sugar daddy*. Dad had just bought her a beautiful new truck and horse trailer, so she was outfitted and ready to go. He was incredibly upset by this announcement and began smoking and drinking even more heavily. He went from drinking a 1.75-liter bottle of bourbon every five days to swilling one down in only three days. This set the stage for what resulted in the beginning of the CareGiver ScareTaker saga.

It was a typical spring evening in April of 2014. Dad turned off the television, finished his last cigarette, and had the last swig of bourbon and water. He wandered into his bedroom and went to sleep for the night. About 6 a.m., he awoke and went outside to pee. He always did that. Who cares? It's a man thing. He was alone in his big house with only the lake in the foreground. It was chilly outside, so he had a lightweight robe on with the waist tie dragging the ground. He began to stumble back toward the sliding glass door, tripped on the threshold, and fell headlong to the floor.

About 7 a.m., one of his friends, Dave, and Dad's farmworker, John, arrived at his house to check their trotlines for catfish. They noticed the outside door to his bedroom was open, so they went in to look around. They found Dad lying on the floor, writhing in pain and bleeding along his leg and hip. They lifted him onto his bed as he was yelling out in pain and tried to make him more comfortable.

They called me. Patrick and I rushed down the hill to manage the situation. The first thing on Dad's mind was that he needed to pee again, but he was in such pain that he could not get up. After several "let 'er go" admonitions, he did. I called 911, and after repeating the address three times and being passed to another operator, an ambulance was summoned. Had he already subscribed to a Life Alert system, the process would have been much easier. This accident was the beginning of our learning experience into the wormhole of senior care. After waiting forty-five minutes, lying on a gurney with a urine- and blood-soaked sheet swaddled around him at the hospital emergency room, he was examined and found to have a fractured right hip. He was sponge bathed, assigned a room, and taken away to surgery. At the time, none of us had really processed the obvious. At eighty-two years old, his days living independently were quickly coming to an end. So, what do you do with your dad immobilized by a broken hip?

During his hospital stay, we had the choice of sneaking alcohol into him or allowing the hospital to detox him. We felt that if he went through the stress of detox medications, he might have a stroke and become further incapacitated, only to come home and start drinking again. He had been through that seven years earlier after having quadruple heart bypass surgery. He returned to all his old habits within days of being released from the hospital.

We chose to sneak alcohol in, but the hospital staff caught on and put him through detox procedures anyway. A nicotine patch and Ativan were administered. He became comatose, suffered a light stroke, and ultimately survived the ordeal. Dad's only real friend, Dave, and I took turns staying with him during his hospital stay.

I want to depart from Dad's story for a moment and help you, the reader, understand why you *must* have an advocate stay with you during hospitalization.

Upon coming out of a coma, therapists began getting Dad up and helping him walk. After a couple of days, the hospitalist was about to discharge him when I noticed his badly distended abdomen. The hospitalist hadn't noticed. I remember the surprised look on his face. An ultrasound was done and Dad was returned to bed with a tube down his throat, draining his stomach. He had developed Ileus, a condition that can be fatal, causing peristalsis (the involuntary wave of contraction and relaxation of the tubular muscular system) to cease and the abdomen to fill up with fluid. He literally almost exploded before the drain began doing its job. Had I not noticed, there wouldn't be a caregiver drama story.

~ * ~

Dad was released, and our first caregiver experience began. It was clear that Dad was incapable of what gerontologists call ADLs, Activities of Daily Living. He couldn't bathe, dress himself, or cook for himself, among other things.

A lovely lady named Mary was hired through an in-home healthcare agency we'll name First Agency. That first caregiver experience was so good. I think it helped us develop the attitude that agencies were doing a fine job of hiring and carefully screening their employees. It turned out this was simply beginner's luck. Mary worked forty hours a week, taking care of Dad. Dad would begin drinking in the late afternoon, just before Mary would leave. These challenges led me to subscribe Dad to a Life Alert service which provided him with a wristwatch-like apparatus with an emergency button. A push of that button would cause the service to call a family member and summon an ambulance. The importance of that device became paramount.

During the next four months, Lisa traveled back and forth doing due diligence concerning moving and buying property, which Dad mostly funded. He became more and more upset because she was moving. One day, in August, when Lisa had not shown up when she had told him she would, he, once again in a drunken stupor, fell and broke the other hip. When Lisa eventually returned, she hit the life alert button. I was called, and an ambulance was summoned. The scenario repeated itself except that this time we asked the hospital staff upfront not to detox him but to prescribe alcohol each day. While they noted that this was unprecedented, they finally agreed to it, given his history. I purchased the alcohol then the hospital pharmacy put it in a prescription bottle, further charging him.

Dave and I returned to our advocacy positions once again. Yes, Lisa, as before, left town the next day. After a week, Dad was released to a skilled care facility. I then learned hospitals no longer bathe patients. Dad was still in his hospital gown when he was transferred to the rehab facility. I helped get him settled in the first day. The next afternoon, I saw him in his wheelchair, and he had not been bathed. I questioned the staff, and even though he wasn't scheduled for that day, they proceeded to finally bathe him that afternoon. He stayed there only three days due to his impatience and erratic behavior, which included screaming, yelling, and pushing the nurse's call button. This behavior was so much that they removed his call button. Because of his other broken hip and drinking, we had to hire caregivers twenty-four hours a day, seven days a week. During this initial attempt to obtain 24/7 care for Dad, our favorite and most honest caregiver, Mary, decided that she needed to help her family more, so she quit.

The first batch of caregivers after Mary was a *revolving door*. One would assume that by hiring an in-home care agency, they would provide qualified people who would 1) show up, 2) arrive on time, and 3) be engaging with the person in their care.

We experienced everything from drug abusers, elder abuse, and extreme laziness to jealousy between caregivers competing for Dad's attention and gifts. Some just couldn't deal with his abusive, drunken, heavy smoking behavior. Kelli was another young woman that was hired. She was kind of a funky girl, with dreads. She was kind of cool and a good cook. We eventually had another woman who was hired, Claire, around my age, early fifties. She arrived on time, was engaging, and had a bright smile. Our family, and Dad, liked her.

Kelli and Claire were two caregivers that were hired, but we still needed a third. The challenges of scheduling and finding caregivers were huge. Two months of the *revolving door* continued. Dad had no appreciation of my help, trying to find the best caregiver for him through First Agency and my share of providing care for him. There was always conflict. Dad's narcissism and selfishness were incredibly difficult to endure.

A typical text message between myself and First Agency went like this:

April 12, 2016:
> "Hi, Jane. Here's what I came up with. Correct me if I'm wrong. Kelli works twenty hours now, right? The addition

of Saturday night through Monday 8 a.m. would be another thirty-eight hours for a total of fifty-eight hours. Let me know what you come up with and other people that might be good."

Jane: "Yes, that's correct. Do you still want her this weekend? Anything over forty hours per worker will be an additional $5/hour. I'm still working on other people and will update you soon."

Me: "For this weekend, we're OK with Kelli. We would like to lower her hours to less than fifty, however. Therefore, you might find someone for Saturday night and half of Sunday. Then, Kelli again the rest of Sunday and Monday. I might back Claire up to noon on Saturday and give her Tuesday night since she's there Tuesday and Wednesday, but that change would begin next weekend."

Next day:

Me: "Kelli is good with this. I still need someone Tuesday – Thursday nights, 6 p.m. to 8 a.m., and Saturday from 6 p.m. to Sunday 4 p.m."

Jane: "OK, that's good to know. Kelli is good. I will add this to her schedule."

Following day:

Jane: "OK, this is the situation. I have a caregiver to work with Jack, but just for this weekend. She can't be there until Sunday at 8 a.m. Actually, Kelli may work, and we'll pay her overtime for the weekend and then, again, next weekend. Then we'll have a new person start."

Are you confused? I was! The goal was to hire three or four caregivers but to have none of them work more than fifty hours a week, minimizing overtime. After much trial and error, we finally ended up with Claire, Kelli, and Dee. Dee was in her late forties, kind of quiet, had a good family. Later, she proved she was one of the better caregivers. The scheduling and personalities seemed to work. However, this cost Dad over $200,000 a year, something few could afford. This was for 24/7 care throughout the year.

~ * ~

Claire began her caregiving job for Dad with enthusiasm. She put on her bright smile and engaging personality and quickly brought happiness to the old gullible patient. The family was very pleased that she encouraged Dad to lower his drinking and smoking. She also helped with farm work, doing as Dad asked and his farmworker, John, needed. Claire and I established excellent communication. She would text me how Dad did with hip therapy, how he was eating, how he was feeling. I was excited she was working out so well, and we even would "work cattle" together when needed. Sometimes, the three of us would out go out for dinner or I was invited to Dad's for supper. *I felt like I had a new friend that I could trust to take care of Dad.*

The first Christmas with Claire, she and I decorated Dad's house. I had found a big red candle to go into a large hanging wreath underneath the covered carport.

Later, I received a text from Claire, "Keep in mind, he is drunk...but he just said, 'After ten years, you all have brought Christmas back to me.' Jacklyn, job well done!"

That made my heart sing!

However, a month later, something began to slightly change. I had overheard a conversation when I was coming into Dad's house one morning. Kelli had made Dad an omelet that he enthusiastically enjoyed, and Dad was praising Kelli's cooking to Claire. So she defiantly made him an omelet.

Claire said, "You better eat every bite of it!"

Chapter 1: Dad's Story

Dad never mentioned Kelli's cooking again. Kelli had taken care of Dad for a few months but left shortly after Claire arrived.

I went through the *revolving door* of caregivers again and after much trial and error, finally ended up with Claire, Terri, and Dee. Terri was in her late twenties and seemed to do a pretty good job.

One day, I noticed a receipt for new tires on Dad's counter. It was for $910. Dad and Claire were gone in his truck. I noticed Claire's car had sparkling new tires. I alerted the family, and we decided that we should call a meeting to confront this situation. The family members were me, my husband, Patrick, and my stepbrother, George, with Dad and Claire.

Much crying ensued and Claire said, "It was just a loan. I promise I'll pay it back!"

Dad was embarrassed that they got caught. We told Claire, if there's anything you need, just let us know.

That meeting turned out to be our greatest mistake concerning Claire. Had we simply called First Agency and had them fire her, that might have been accomplished. However, we gave her another chance. It was just so difficult to find good, dependable caregivers, even when enlisting an agency!

Unbeknownst to us, this gave Claire more time to secure her place with Dad. Before long, she was digging her hooks deeper into his emotional, *wanted to be needed state*. She exercised a most pernicious influence over him. Firing her was no longer an option. Dad would rehire her as a private caregiver and settle any non-compete charges from First Agency.

Dad chose to spend most holidays with Lisa rather than his family. After Lisa moved away, Claire began taking Dad to her mother and stepfather's house in a town two hours away. They gladly welcomed him into their home, proclaiming their appreciation because he was "taking care of their little girl." It struck me strange that this con artist I was learning to know came from a rather well-off family who lived in a nice home on a lake and had a boat. They didn't need Dad, but Claire certainly did.

Claire, Dad, and his dog, Josey, would go fishing near the area of her parents. Dad and Claire's relationship continued to grow and any monitoring we attempted drove them further underground. A conversation between them might go like this:

"What do you need, Jack Foster"?

"What?" he'd respond.

"What do you need?" she yelled!

"Toothpick." he answered.

"Wrong answer," was her haughty reply. "You need *me*!"

"Well, yes I do," he replied.

While working very hard and doing many more tasks than the average caregiver, she was gaining control of his mind. She was brainwashing him. Even two years after her hiring, I overheard her yell, "No one can take care of you like I do." She was relentless in getting and maintaining control of his needy mind.

"Whatcha doing, Jack Foster?"

"We're going to your house when we get through buying groceries," he replied. "We'll see where you want your new carport."

"Let's do it," the excited Claire added.

Jack boasted, "I've got $700 – $800 to spend on you!"

Another day, Claire would tell him loudly, "My other job said March 13, set your clocks one hour ahead."

He responded, "What? Time change?"

"I'll do it Saturday night before I leave. You don't think anybody else would set them ahead for you, do you?" Claire said while adjusting the clocks.

"Hell no," he replied.

"Ever?"

"Ever." he replied.

"I'll take care of it before I leave on Saturday, Jack Foster. That way, when you get up on Sunday, you'll be right on time. Anyone else give a shit about you?"

"Hell no!" he replied.

~ * ~

Chapter 1: Dad's Story

I began to notice that First Agency's billings were inflated and incorrect. As it turned out, their billing agent was embezzling money and inflating each client's statement enough to cover up her theft! I knew the owner, so when I posed billing questions, I would copy him. I saved them a lot of future problems by exposing the bookkeeper's fraud. What a mess it was to sort out regarding the billing! The billing agent was escorted out in handcuffs. It seems that the caregiving industry is fraught with fraud from all sides. Dad's three caregivers, Dee, Claire, and Terri, transferred to a new agency, "Second Agency."

The owners of Second Agency evaluated Dad, met the family, so it seemed like this was a good start.

Dad had a beautiful red female heeler named Cinnamon. She had passed away before Dad needed in-home care. He had her cremated and her ashes were in a small cedar box with her name on it. One day while Claire and I were working cattle, she mentioned that her cat had died over the weekend and that it had been a tough ordeal. I sympathized with her. A week later, I visited Dad and didn't see Cinnamon's box on the hallway desk. I asked Terri where the box was. She didn't know but she told me that Dad had said that he and Claire had scattered Cinnamon's ashes the previous week.

I texted Claire, asking if she knew what happened to Cinnamon's cedar box. No response, but it appeared on the hallway desk a week later, empty. This woman had used dad's dog cremation box for her cat!!

Once Claire secured her position with Dad, she didn't mind telling a friend and me that she had been in jail for meth. I even found her picture on "Mugshots.com" online shortly after that. Are you kidding me?? How did this happen? How did she ever get hired? We had believed that agencies did a good job of screening their applicants. Oh, and that beautiful smile? Her teeth weren't real! Meth addicts rarely have good teeth! There was nothing I or any family member could do. I mentioned this to the owner of Second Agency. He showed me her record on his computer screen and replied, "Well, you know, we inherited her from First Agency."

Meaning, I had requested Claire to transfer from First Agency, but I didn't know she had a jail record until she told me!

It was a no-win situation. Nothing compared to the challenges of dealing with the dishonest and con artist persona of Claire. Dad was convinced and brainwashed that Claire was "his girl" and nobody would get in their way. She made him feel special, all because of the money.

The "real" Claire also showed up in her poor judgment. There were accidents with Dad's truck. Various dents, and the colliding mirrors accident on a narrow bridge between his and another truck. The diesel exhaust fluid (DEF) warning light came on; Dad asked her to put in the DEF fluid. She put it in the gas tank instead of the opening for the DEF additive. This one cost Dad $12,000 and, not long after, the price of a new diesel pickup.

According to Dee, I learned that Dad had paid for Claire's grandchildren's summer camp, had given her and her cousin three calves, and, of course, the carport. He also paid off the $22,000 balance on her rent-to-own house, and then had to hire an attorney to secure the deed since the landlord had never had anyone pay him off before! The list goes on. Dad owned a mobile home on one of his farms; he rented it to Claire's son, charging him rent, but then giving the rent money back to Claire. She never directly asked for money, just mention a need and whine about it; *the money tree will shake.*

His monthly grocery expenses exceeded $600, and he rarely ate at home. He would buy her groceries and cartons of cigarettes. "You're a grown-ass man! If you wanna smoke—smoke!"

If you succeed in deceiving someone, don't think that person is a fool. It's just that the person trusted you more than you deserve.

Claire texted me one morning that I needed to come to Dad's house immediately. It was a rarity to speak with her anymore since I knew who and what she was. And she knew I knew.

I am cautious in telling this story because of its intimate nature, which some adult children are familiar with, having to give their parent

Chapter 1: Dad's Story

an enema. I arrived and Claire told me Dad had not had a bowel movement in three days. He was in the bathroom. I asked him if he wanted to go to the doctor; he refused. I asked him if he wanted an ambulance; he refused. There was one enema. Claire mentioned she would do it but would be in trouble because she's not licensed for medical care. I replied there was more she could be in trouble for.

Well, I did what I could do, then went on to work as my day was filled with appointments. I told Claire to keep me posted as the day went on.

I had a business lunch, then another meeting. Claire tried to reach me and I returned her call once I had a few minutes. Claire called my brother, Ty, and Ty had to summon an ambulance. After discussion with my brother, why didn't Claire just hit the Life Alert button to summon the ambulance?

When I arrived at the hospital, Ty and Claire were outside an emergency room cubicle where Dad was. While we were waiting on the nurses, I looked down and noticed Claire had very beautiful, manicured toenails—a "pedi"! They were prettier than my toenails! Why was that? When she would take Dad to a nail salon to get his nails clipped, of course, she would get a "mani/pedi" also!

The nurses proceeded to manually de-compact Dad. That woke him up from his snooze! Once he was transferred to a hospital room, Claire went to the house to get a change of clothes and get us something to eat. She returned with three burgers, fries, and sodas! What?? Why would she think Dad could eat? After this ordeal, he couldn't eat anything!

By the way, do not feed someone solid foods, like pork chops or steaks, when they haven't had a bowel movement in three days! I checked his refrigerator and threw out a leftover pork chop, corn on the cob and pecan pie. Why is he eating this stuff while he's constipated? I thought to myself. I subsequently learned that part of the daily care sheet was never filled out. After that incident, I made sure it was.

Some people have noticed that Claire bends over inches away from Dad, exposing her breasts. Might she be showing him her body? We had

17

noticed a few times that she had forgotten to put her dentures back in her mouth. What a sight that was! Dad's jeans were also sometimes unbuttoned and unzipped. Is some sort of oral sex happening? Dave and John would see them kiss each other when she was leaving or kiss each other feverishly when Dave was taking Dad for a short trip. Dad would call her every single day. Claire was involved in and taking control of every aspect of Dad's life. She always made sure that his doctor's appointments were during her shift, even if it meant delaying his care. On one occasion, when he needed surgery to remove plaque from the arteries in his legs, I noticed his appointments were being delayed by almost six months to accommodate her schedule. I took it upon myself to make the pre-surgery appointment happen ASAP, regardless of the day. Of course, she complained to Dad that I had changed the appointment solely to prevent her from going, thus further corrupting his mind to turn him against me. She was as narcissistic as he was!

After Dad returned home from the leg surgery, he remained on the couch to sleep. It was very difficult for him to get up. In fact, he couldn't. He also had a catheter. Claire had retired to the back bedroom for the evening. "I'm going to pray you sleep well, Jack!"

Dad was coughing and hacking and in pain, lying on the living room couch.

"What's all that racket?!" Claire yelled.

Dad responded, "I'm sorry."

*

Dad had some guys that stayed at his house every year during a huge motorcycle rally. That day came, and Claire was on duty. The three motorcycle riders left a bottle of whiskey on the counter and told Jack that they would have a drink with him after spending a few hours at the rally. While they were gone, Dad drank the entire bottle, got up from his chair, and fell to the floor. Claire was on duty while Dad was getting drunk and did nothing to stop him. This fall did not break anything; it just gave him a few cuts and bruises. However, as the night went on, he began having extreme pain near his collar bone, so off to the emergency room he went.

Chapter 1: Dad's Story

The attending physician determined that Dad had severely burned his esophagus. The doctor explained to him that if he ever took another drink, his esophagus would rupture and that it would kill him.

The whole event must have really scared him because he went through the horrible drama and hallucinations of detox and has remained sober. Interestingly, sobriety did not change his mean and volatile nature. Dad was in the hospital for a couple of weeks but mostly recovered and came home to resume what had become his normal life. No sodas, no alcohol, but continued to smoke.

I had heard that he and Claire were going on a trip to Houston to visit his ailing and demented sister, Joy. She had lived in Oklahoma, but in the last years, moved to Texas to live with her daughter's family, and they became her caregivers. I told Dad, "Well, maybe I would like to go and visit Aunt Joy and cousin Holle." After some disagreeable conversation, Dad reluctantly and angrily agreed to take me to Houston instead of Claire. The days leading up to the trip were filled with malice and ill will. He called me the morning of the trip and said the trip was off because he didn't have the tickets. I told him I had printed the tickets with my computer the night before. He hung up on me. He hung up on me a few times. I called him and asked why he was hanging up on me?? "I'm done talking!" he yelled.

I knew he was upset that I was going instead of Claire. This was all her idea anyway. I called Claire and told her to call him to calm him down and explain that tickets are not mailed anymore. She told me he had called her at 5:30 that morning. Dee ended up driving us to the airport. So much for a little father/daughter time.

I got him in a wheelchair at the airport and on the plane. Even with first-class tickets and a short distance to the restroom, it just wasn't close enough. Well, you know. It was a mess when we arrived in Houston.

~*~

In 2017, Dad and Claire discussed what he wanted to do for his eighty-fifth birthday. He replied, "I'd like to go to Jackson Hole, Wyoming, one more time to feed the elk."

They decided they would go in celebration of his eighty-fifth birthday the following February. The U.S. Forest Service no longer allows tourist feeding, but one can go on a horse-drawn wagon and watch hundreds of them feed, fight, and whatever else they do.

Claire first thought that she and Dad would go, but Claire realized that didn't look good. So Claire thought of planning a big family trip. Dad asked George to handle the details of the trip. In the end, twenty-four family members went. Dad chartered two jet airplanes, flew Aunt Joy and Holle to Jackson Hole from Texas, rented most of a motel, bought meals, and provided a van for local transportation. The whole affair seemed a bit like herding cats, but the group of relatives got along better than expected.

Upon returning, Claire boasted to her company and the other caregivers that her client had spent $70K on this trip, and she was the only caregiver invited to go. She loved showing Dee and Terri the gifts that Dad had bought for her. Her boastful words turned out to be a huge red flag at Second Agency and irritated everyone.

A few days after returning from the elk trip, Second Agency called a meeting with me, my brother, and stepbrother. They had already met with the other two caregivers, Terri and Dee, regarding the trip and other incidents with Claire. The agency owners read a list of complaints, suspicions, and a few provable accusations to Claire, and she did her usual. She burst into tears and compliantly promised to correct all her transgressions. Ultimately, she signed an agreement stating that she would stop speaking negatively about other caregivers, stop accepting money and gifts, promptly notify me of any health issues with Dad, and a whole list of other regulations. This included Dee driving Dad to see Claire at her house on her days off! The Incident Report and Warning Notice reveals the extent of the travesties involved.

Chapter 1: Dad's Story

Incident Report

Re: Claire—, Caregiver to Jack

Date: February 10, 2017

The following violations of the Standards of Conduct/Ethical Behavior signed contract at Second Agency Senior Care have been reported regarding the care of client, Jack. These accusations regarding caregiver, Claire, have been reported by Jack's caregivers: Terri and Dee.

The Standards of Conduct Violations reported include the following:

Standard 3. Talking negatively about co-workers, client family or client representative. Claire has repeatedly spoken negatively about Jack's family members in the presence of Jack, as well as in the presence of the caregivers. Examples: "Jack, your family is so evil...Jacklyn is so evil." "No one cares about you except me." "Your family members never come to see you." "Your family does not care about you, especially Jacklyn." "The other caregivers never clean, I'm the only one who works around here."

Standard 4. Accepting gifts from the client or the client's family...this includes gifts from the client to the caregiver's children, relatives or caregiver's friends. A. Claire has received up to 7 calves from Jack for herself or her family members. B. She has also had her tires paid for by Jack—over $900, C. a lawyer fee of $4,000 paid for by Jack. D. Christmas presents she shopped for to give to her family members paid for by Jack. E. Claire's son rents a trailer from Jack and gets his rent refunded in cash either to Claudia or her son—Jack has mentioned "cash back" on $400 rent to her son. F. Expense paid trip to Wyoming—not approved by the office.

Standard 12. <u>Maintaining a personal relationship outside of work with the client</u>. When Claire is not at work, she calls Jack several times during the day. She also has Jack over to her house several times in a month, requesting the caregivers bring Jack to come see her and her family (also a violation of Standard 27).

Standard 13. <u>Making changes to care plan without talking to Care Coordinator</u>. Often Claire bargains with the other caregivers to get more of their hours, often making them feel bad if they don't agree to give them to her. She makes Jack schedule his doctor appointments around her work schedule, thus delaying his care.

Standard 14. <u>Offering medical advice</u>. Claire has been known on two occasions to differ with John regarding his opinion of what to do medically for the cattle. The cattle are his responsibility. For instance: when John decided a calf wasn't going to make it, Claire insisted they take it to the vet anyway. The calf died 12 hours later. A similar situation happened with another sick calf. This is completely out of Claire's domain and authority.

Standard 19. <u>Borrowing money or other items from the client</u>. Claire has been known to "borrow" food, equipment, and money from Jack.

Standard 23. <u>Bringing visitors or pets to the client's home</u>. Claire's family members (children, grandchildren, etc.) are frequently at the house. No one in the agency has been asked if she can bring them there.

Standard 26. <u>Visiting the client during off-duty time</u> without prior approval from the office or client rep. Claire has made strict requirements that Jack cannot go to the doctor, the bank, or the sale barn without her. Often she has to visit Jack during off-duty time to do this.

Standard 31. Discussing personal problems, financial difficulties, health problems with the client. It is common knowledge amongst caregivers that Claire discusses personal issues with Jack. Example: A. When Claire's grandson was having open-heart surgery, Jack repeatedly tried to call Claire, leaving her voicemails asking how the baby was doing. He was overburdened by worry and concern. But Claire didn't return his calls. B. On Feb. 7, Jack complained to Dee that he was up worrying all night about Claire because Second Agency had reduced the number of hours Claire worked. He must have learned this from Claire, and Claire must have caused him to worry that she was going to have to get more hours or leave him.

Standard 33. Getting involved in the client financial matters. It is inappropriate for the caregivers to be involved in any way with the financial affairs of the client. Examples: Claire knows where Jack's "cash stash" is, but the family members do not. Claire insists on handling all the banking with Jack. Since so many of Jack's transactions are done in cash, it puts Claire in a vulnerable position to be accused of theft or other methods of self-gain.

Standard 34. Accepting additional employment with the client outside the scope of the care plan. Claire and several of her family members have accepted jobs on the ranch outside of caregiving.

Emotional/Psychological Abuse (pg 17): intimidation, manipulation, threats, verbal assaults, instilling fear of any kind toward the client. Claire has used manipulation by saying to Jack repeatedly, "The only person you can trust is me," "Your family doesn't care about you, only I care about you," "I will be here with you until you die," etc. Claire has also been known to yell at Jack or chew him out by saying, "Jack, you don't appreciate anything I do."

Client Banking (pg. 17) "In most situations, performing banking transactions for your client is prohibited. This includes check cashing, online banking, and ATM transactions. Client banking will be allowed when prior authorization has been given from Second Agency Senior Care. Whenever a caregiver is given cash for shopping, groceries or any purchase, the caregiver must give the client a receipt along with the correct change, then complete the Agency's money management form in the client notebook. Take a picture of the receipt with your phone as a second form of proof and text to the office." Note: Claire has rarely, if ever, turned in receipts for purchases. She should have permission from the office if she is going to do purchasing or banking for Jack.

~ * ~

Second Agency Senior Care
Employee Warning Notice

Date: February 22, 2017

Employee Name: Claire—

1) Your behavior/actions have been found unsatisfactory in the following areas:

A. Insubordination through at least 14 violations of Second Agency's Standard of Conduct & Ethics as listed in the Second Agency's Handbook.

Chapter 1: Dad's Story

2) The following corrective immediate/sustained actions must be taken by the employee:

(A) Claire is not to fill Jack's pill/med tray. This is Jacklyn's responsibility or whomever she designates to fill the tray.

(B) Claire is not to talk to client regarding her work schedule concerns (as this causes him stress). Claire is to handle all scheduling concerns with the Agency Scheduler.

(C) Claire is not to be involved in the scheduling of Jack's doctor appointments or medical care unless Jacklyn has given permission for Claire to do so. Claire is then to communicate all appointments with Jacklyn.

(D) Claire is not to plan trips, parties or other events for Jack without first consulting with Second Agency. The Agency will then consult with Jacklyn or George.

(E) Claire is not to have any responsibility regarding the care and maintenance of Jack's cattle. Worker's Comp. insurance will not cover her.

(F) Claire is not to speak negatively to the client, Jack, about his family members.

(G) Claire is not to speak negatively to the client, Jack, about other caregivers or the staff at Second Agency Senior Care.

(H) Claire is not to share her own or her family's personal problems with the client. This includes but is not limited to her or her family's health problems, financial problems, emotional problems, work issues, etc. This causes undue stress and anxiety upon the client.

(I) Claire is no longer to accept gifts nor financial gifts from client.

(J) Claire is no longer to borrow items from client.

(K) Claire is no longer to have Jack visit her home or her family's homes.

(L) Claire is no longer to have her family members to Jack's home without securing permission from Second Agency.

(M) Claire is not to visit client when she is off shift from the Agency.

(N) Claire is not to be involved in any way regarding any of Jack's financial transactions, including but not limited to: banking, check cashing, transfer of funds, receipt of cash for sell of cattle or other items.

(O) Claire is no longer to make grocery purchases, meal purchases, or any purchases for Jack without turning in a receipt to Second Agency.

(P) Claire is not allowed to give financial advice to Jack nor in anyway be involved in the financial affairs.

(Q) Claire is to have no contact with Jack, outside of work unless there has been permission given from Second Agency.

(R) Claire is to refrain from using phrases on the client which implies she is the only one he can trust, or that she is the only one who cares about him.

(S) Claire is to refrain from making threats to quit the client if she does not get the schedule she wants.

(T) Claire is not to have Jack call Second Agency's office regarding her schedule. Claire is to call the office herself regarding her schedule.

(U) Claire is not to make schedule changes with other caregivers. Claire is to let Second Agency Scheduler handle all schedule change requests.

3. Failure to comply in these corrective measures will result in the immediate termination of the employee.

Your signature on this form means that we have discussed the situation and that you agree to comply with the corrective measures required.

Employee Signature: _____

Date: _____

Manager Signature: _____

Date: _____

Firing Claire was discussed, but we could not because Dad would go around us, hire her privately and possibly remove us from his estate, namely, me. I was the one closest to him and he believed I was the one causing the problems! Second Agency was also aware that they would likely lose his very large cash account by firing Claire. It seems integrity only applies when there are no consequences. After all, they had hired her as a contract employee, knowing she had a prison record.

Reflecting, these stressful days and meetings produced the same results of other crisis periods—they simply drove Dad and Claire further underground. Consequently, nothing of substance changed.

In fact, Terri quit. How could she continue to work for Second Agency in the face of all she knew about what was going on with Claire? Terri was replaced by Renee.

~ * ~

Renee gave the best care to Dad. Dee, Renee, and Claire became the longest-term caregiver threesome. Renee did not have a vibrant personality, but more importantly, she was kind, honest, and ethical. She took good care of him and was reliable. She was with Dad for almost three years. She never accepted his $100 bills or other bribes for affection. That did not sit well with him because it didn't stroke his ego or make him feel needed.

Renee didn't like conflict and seemed like a loner. Though she frequently seemed depressed, she always took compassionate care of both my parents. She truly cared for my mom and dad.

Claire eventually began criticizing Renee. That was her repeating pattern. She built herself up by tearing others down. Renee was leaving one day and gave John a hug goodbye. Claire then quipped to John, "You're not going to have that nasty old thing hug ya, are ya?" He just looked down and walked away.

~ * ~

A year had passed and I noticed that Dad's beloved dog, Josey, was vomiting frequently. Renee called me and we took Josey to the emergency veterinarian clinic, where they kept him overnight. The next day, we took him to his regular veterinarian. In the evening, we would pick up Josey and return him to the emergency vet clinic. After the second evening, he was diagnosed with pancreatitis. Dad approved him to have surgery and we went home.

Josey, being twelve years old and thirty pounds overweight, passed away during the surgery attempting to repair a rupture in his colon. The vet called and told me the sad news. I went to Dad's house to give him the bad news. Dad couldn't hear well because he never would wear his hearing aids.

I said, "Josey died!"

Dad said, "Birthday?!"

I said, "No! Josey died!" in a much stronger voice.

Upon hearing that, he began sobbing and screaming.

The ensuing drama led to a huge altercation between Dad and me. I told Dad and Claire that this had been preventable! Meaning, the caregivers always gave Josey table scraps that caused him to be so overweight. I left. Claire was there and convinced Dad that I blamed him for Josey's death. She twisted my words. I never blamed Dad.

Chapter 1: Dad's Story

I know this because Ty came to my house an hour later and was calling DHS on me for elder abuse!? Claire had called him and told him that I had verbally abused Dad. Geesh!

The next day, I heard Dad was so upset that he demanded that Dave pick up Josey's body from the vet clinic and put him in a deep freezer. There was going to be a funeral. All of this was Claire's idea. She took Dad to a local funeral home, where he bought a vault, an adult-sized human casket, and began planning a funeral. She had taken Dad to the monument company to order a headstone. I learned from Dee that Josey was going to be spelled "Josie" on the headstone! Oh, heck no! Josey had originally been my dog, which I let Dad have years earlier. I named him Josey, after the outlaw, Josey Wales. Not a girl's name! Dee, Dad, and I went to breakfast one morning and we stopped by the monument company so I could correct the spelling.

A preacher was hired, chairs were set up, and we had a humanlike funeral near a tree in his yard. Dave put Josey's toys in the casket and I added Cinnamon's empty cedar box. At one point, Dad became so grief-stricken that he attempted to climb into the casket with his dog. It was quite a drama.

~ * ~

Over a few years, I had become acquainted with the owners of Second Agency, even somewhat considered them friends. They had even attended Josey's funeral and had taken pictures of Dad and I together. It was heartfelt. They seemed genuine and caring. However, after all my monitoring and complaining about Claire and the situation, nothing was ever done. They listened well, expressed empathy, but did absolutely nothing. I just thought they were not aware of Claire's manipulations.

I learned later that I was so wrong. Second Agency would do whatever Claire wanted them to do. The inmate was running the asylum!

On one of the trips that Dad and Claire took to go fishing, Dad had fallen. He had a leg cramp, got up, and fell over a chair. He ended up with a black eye and bruised lip. He didn't want to go to a doctor and they went on fishing. Claire reported the incident to Second Agency and the family, but Dad didn't want her to know how much pain he was in, fearing she would be blamed.

A week later, he complained to Dee and Renee that he was in pain. Only then was he taken to the doctor and x-rayed. Renee thought there might be a small compression fracture. Dad let Dee and Renee know when his back hurt or when he was in pain. He didn't let Claire know how much pain because he didn't want her to be blamed or feel bad for his fall on her duty.

Renee slept on a love seat near Dad, who slept on a couch, in the living room. She was terrified that he might fall. She awakened every hour or so, checking on him and taking him to the bathroom. She assisted him every step of the way.

A weekend before Christmas, she had fallen and hurt her back. She called Dad to say she couldn't come to work. (A dire mistake. She should have called Second Agency.) Her voice was subdued and he couldn't understand her, so he handed the telephone to Claire. She took the phone, listened to Renee, and afterward announced to Dad that Renee was drunk.

She exclaimed, "She's always drunk! She doesn't take good care of you. I don't know why she is still here!"

The following Monday, Dee drove Dad to Second Agency and Dad, in Jack Foster form, announced he didn't want "that drunk" in his house and if she showed up, he would send her home. Renee was fired from Second Agency. I know this because I called Renee and she related the details to me. Claire had found the perfect opportunity to get rid of Renee.

Dad had fallen twice during Claire's shifts, but never during Renee's. Claire always slept in the back bedroom. Renee, always near Dad.

Renee passed away five months later at age fifty-one. She had been taking a lot of pain meds and was very depressed. We don't know if she overdosed or what happened. The details of her passing were not made available. Dad didn't even seem to remember her when Dee and I showed him Renee's obituary.

Chapter 1: Dad's Story

~ * ~

Dad was so skinny, I could feel his shoulder blades when I gave him a hug. Most mornings, Dad wanted the caregiver on duty to take him to a breakfast place, where Claire's ex-jail mate worked and would coo over him. This way, Claire had a "watchful eye" over Dad. He had ceased wanting to go to other breakfast diners he used to go to previously.

What eventually "broke my camel's back" was I found grocery receipts totaling $300 in an eight-day period in January 2020. I had taken pictures of the three receipts and texted Claire asking if they had enough groceries to last a while. She never responded.

Claire must have "harped," or "nagged" on Dad about my review of the receipts, and she convinced him that I was after his money. Dee told me those groceries "walked out the door." Claire also didn't like me picking up the daily care sheets on a weekly basis, reviewing them and making notes on them before I turned them into Second Agency. I didn't want another episode like what had happened previously when Dad became constipated. Claire would mail the care sheets to the agency. Honestly, I don't know if Second Agency ever did review the care sheets!

A month later, Dad removed me as his primary POA for healthcare. Ty and George took my place. They both live thirty minutes away. There was never a discussion nor explanation. George called Patrick to let us know I had been removed. Dad had Claire dial the attorney's number and Dad told his attorney to draw up the paperwork and it was done.

Who did this really hurt? Dad. Who did this really help? Claire. She was now not being "watched" and forged a better bond with my brother, who didn't question the reasoning of this.

~ * ~

In March 2020, Patrick and I received an email from George. Because of COVID-19, everyone was advised to have limited or no visitation with Dad. And there was going to be a change of schedule. I broke "protocol" to see Dad the evening I received the email.

Claire had left at 4 p.m. and would return at 4 p.m. the next day, to be on full shift for two weeks. What a Grand Scheme! She had called Dee the prior morning and spoke about more money for herself if she could secure a leave of absence from her other job. Claire would be the one, and only one, to care for Dad during this perilous time!

When I walked through Dad's front door, the main wooden door was open, with the glass door closed. This is winter and, of course, Dad pays the electric bill. I walked in and Kaylee, a new caregiver, was on her phone, then hanging up from a personal call. She was on the other side of the room, out of eyesight of Dad. She then approached me to shake my hand! I refused.

I approached Dad and let him know I loved him. He said he loved me too. I asked if he knew I loved him; he said yes. I told him I couldn't see him for the next few weeks and that Ty and Claire didn't want me to see him. He said nothing. I teared up, told him I loved him, and left.

So, my question: When Claire returns the next day, after all her running around to get things in order to camp at Dad's for two weeks, would she be screened for the virus before she entered Dad's house? No! Was Kaylee tested for the virus before entering Dad's house? No!

Dee was fired during this time because she exposed all the texts and truth about Claire to the administrator of Second Agency. Just too problematic, so they fired her! By the way, Dad never fell on her watch either. I had lunch with Dee and offered to go to the local police with her. She spoke with the police over the phone, she spoke with the prosecuting attorney and other attorneys. Nobody would do anything. It was because all of this was "Dad's decisions." Well, you know who was behind every decision!

Dad fell in late April 2020 under Kaylee's care. He called me and I rushed to his house in minutes. When I arrived, Kaylee had Dad's jacket around him to keep him warm. I removed his jacket, placed a hand towel under his T-shirt, and covered him with two bath towels to keep him warm. He seemed hurt around his collarbone area. I rinsed the blood out of his jacket liner.

Chapter 1: Dad's Story

Ty arrived two hours later and the in-home care nurse arrived an hour after Ty. I told Dad I could have him at the ER within a half hour if he let me. He just sat there. While I sat with Dad for those hours, I asked him why he removed me as his Health POA. He said I was after his money. I told him I didn't need his money. His reply was, "I know that." How do I argue with that, my dad, when he is in pain? I just let it go. However, the change remained. Now that I no longer am Dad's POA, all communication between me and Second Agency has ceased. An important lesson is: *do not befriend either the caregivers or the agency you are using*. I must say, though, after six years of doing the job, my life is calmer. I'm not *on alert* or being defensive with Dad.

As one reads these many scenarios of drama and fraud as he moves from manic bravado and delusion to depressive anger and abuse of his family and caregivers, it becomes painfully clear that his way of living creates great pain in those around him. He has lived a life of loaning needy people money, then angrily demanding that it be repaid, usually without success. Now he is the victim of other needy people, and he is so incapacitated and needy himself that he doesn't recognize the fraud. His caregiver, now entitled **ScareTaker**, has taken him for quite a ride.

~ * ~

Many seniors, especially wealthy seniors who have the entitled sense that they are special and deserve the extra attention, are being preyed upon by unethical and cajoling con artists. I was unaware. I naively thought hiring an in-home care agency would be the best thing to do. They should have the responsibility and liability to interview and hire good, honest caregivers. Yes, I discussed suing Second Agency. I would lose because all of this has been "dad's decisions". A year has passed since being removed as Healthcare POA. Dad has never called me since he first fell. I'm sure he was instructed by Claire to never call me. He never has the other caregivers drive him by my house. I see him only a few minutes a week, at his house, when I bring him the Sunday paper. We get along better because I only see him for a few minutes each week. Dad can no longer blame me for his unhappy days, and I have resolved not to worry about him so much. I learned I just couldn't care as much. At times, the look on his face shows that he's angry to be alive, but afraid to die.

After Dad fell the fourth time, in Kaylee's care, he broke his elbow. This is after he had staples in his head from a fall in December! I called the owners of Second Agency. We had not spoken in more than a year due to my POA removal, and because of that, they reminded me that HIPPA rules prevented them from speaking to me about Dad's care. I told them I didn't need to know anything about Dad's care, but I asked them if they knew Dad had fallen four times under Kaylee's care in the past year. I could tell by their response that they did not. I told them I'd be damned if she returned to take care of my dad anymore. She did not. Dad lays in the bed he has made and no telling how much more money Claire has taken from him.

I visited Dad when he returned home from the hospital after the elbow surgery. There was a new caregiver there. He was lying in a hospital bed in the living room watching tv. A new caregiver was sitting in a chair behind him. I noticed his stomach was exposed due to him lying on his unbuttoned wrinkled t-shirt and shirt. I pulled his shirts up and around him to cover his stomach. His hand was resting on a pillow, his elbow was in a downward position. I gently removed the pillow from under his hand and placed it under his elbow, since it needs to be elevated after surgery. Why am I doing this? How do I know this? Why hasn't this been done by the caregiver??

~ * ~

In the last week of Dad's life, I was told he had suffered a stroke on Saturday. I went to see him Sunday afternoon, after Claire left her shift. When I walked in, I heard him groaning, yelling. Miffy, a caregiver was texting on her phone sitting behind his hospital bed in the living room. When I approached him, his mouth was open, he had "dry mouth". I immediately asked Miffy if there was something to moisten his mouth. She returned with a moistened towelette. His mouth just grabbed onto that, to moisten his dry lips. He needed it.

Chapter 1: Dad's Story

He was laying kind of crooked with his chin pushing into his chest. I asked Miffy if we could either lay him down or prop him up a little more. We propped him up. Again, even in the last week of his life, we were still plagued with inadequate caregivers. I rubbed his hair and kissed him on the forehead. He winked at me to let me know he recognized me.

On Tuesday I visited him briefly. This time there was a small bowl of water with the pink sponge tip in it to continually moisten his lips. I rubbed his head lightly, his hair, and kissed his forehead. I put my hand on his hand. He raised up my hand and kissed it. I kissed him on the cheek and told him it was ok to go and that I loved him very much. That was the last time I saw him alive.

~ * ~

Reflecting, Dad had lost his hearing years earlier and purchased numerous hearing aids, but never liked them. I've learned there is an association between hearing loss and dementia. My Aunt Joy and Dad's mother both had been diagnosed with dementia. Dad never was. It would've been helpful to have a mental competency exam done, beginning at age eighty. It would have provided a baseline for mental clarity.

Secondly, most in-home care agency rates hover around $20 per hour. The caregiver is typically paid around minimum wage. Note, this is an in-home caregiver, not a Certified Nursing Assistant. CNA's, unfortunately, are paid around the same minimum wage. The in-home care person can assist the senior with Activities of Daily Living (ADLs). As I was told by one of the caregivers, "I'm not familiar with wound care" after Dad had fallen.

The terms "home care" and "home health" seem similar, but they provide distinctly different services. Home care offers nonclinical help, such as meal prep and companionship, while home health provides professional medical assistance. Another difference is that home health is generally covered by Medicare or private insurance while home care is not.

If an in-home care agency does not accept Medicaid, then there is not oversight by Department of Human Services.

~ * ~

Now, let me transition into what I am working on to improve the situation for others. I am a reluctant expert in many of the situations that surround senior care. Because of the situations I have encountered, my *passion* is Senior Care Advocate.

My profession is Commercial Real Estate. I am a licensed broker and CCIM, Certified Commercial Investment Member, in both Texas and Arkansas. When renewing my Texas broker's license in early 2020, I had to complete extra paperwork in addition to my continuing education requirements. I was required to sign off on the FBI's Rap Back program. I thought, what's this? I researched the program and why Texas requires participation. FBI Rap Back is a real-time, ongoing background check. More than a yearly or one-time check, it is an ongoing, real-time background check.

Think of it this way. If a caregiver were arrested for drug violations but had a good job, they might be able to arrange a little time off from work to go to court and deal with the issue. The employer would never know. However, with an ongoing and real-time background check, the state police would notify the employer. This was implemented because the Texas Real Estate Commission became aware that felons were involved in real estate transactions! Upon this writing, only six states have implemented the FBI Rap Back program. Also, being licensed in Real Estate, I have been fingerprinted in both Texas and Arkansas. Most states do not require licensing of the agency or that the caregivers are fingerprinted. They should be background checked and drug tested also.

I contacted four legislators before finally getting one's ear. House Representative Clint Penzo was familiar with some problems surrounding caregiving because of his own family trials. He wrote House Bill 1585 that became a law July 2021. It will require new applicants of certain healthcare providers to have a criminal background check and fingerprinting. This will affect providers of personal services to daycare, teen facilities, and senior care. The FBI Rap Back program was discussed but not pursued. It is not enough, as *all* caregivers need to be fingerprinted and to implement the FBI Rap Back program, but it is a start.

Another House Representative, Carlton Wing, wrote House Bill 1391 that became a law July 2021. This will allow financial services providers, such as banks, to either refuse or delay executing financial transactions involving suspected financial exploitation of elderly or disabled people. The banks want to protect their customers and their assets!

My website, *www.caregiverscaretakers.com* offers many resources. You can review Resources and find a site to hire a caregiver directly, avoiding an agency. You can pay for a background check and check references to issue a 1099 to them at the end of the year.

I find better-qualified caregivers from my online sources than paying an agency $20 plus, an hour. You can save yourself $5 – $10 an hour handling things yourself. The actual caregivers earn more, and you pay less. Be prepared to issue a 1099 to them for their "independent contractor" status of employment.

This is a huge and growing problem that is not going to go away! This is not a situation that always comes to us with good warning. It frequently occurs as part of a crisis that is completely unexpected. We think that we are dealing with agencies that truly care. Well, because of my experiences, I have mixed feelings. However, if you find a qualified, caring, and ethical caregiver, treat them like *gold* because they are!

Chapter 2

Mom's Story

Mom's story began with a cancer diagnosis when she was in her 70's. First was colon cancer and then breast cancer. Colon cancer reappeared in her liver and then later her abdomen.

On March 31, 2017, she began experiencing excruciating pain in her stomach, so she went to the emergency room. The doctor on duty, after much waiting and a few tests, informed us that she had a perforated bowel and that she had only hours, or maybe a few days, to live. So, he sent her to a nearby hospice facility. After a few days, the perforation healed, and she was released to her home, where the hospice program could administer their protocol in the few remaining months she had to live. The six months before she passed were filled with caregivers, me, and Susan.

Susan and I had to immediately make arrangements to be away from our homes and make adjustments to the schedules of our lives.

I needed to activate Mom's long-term care insurance policy and hire a home health care agency. I had experience dealing with agencies when arranging care for my dad. My parents had been divorced for around 50 years.

I called two other agencies in addition to Second Agency that was caring for Dad. Because these other agencies paid their employees more money, I thought we would get better quality care. So, the caregiver journey began (again).

The agency, whom I have since renamed "Hell Cometh," recommended Lisa as our first caregiver. She was scheduled to come four eight-hour days and two four-hour shifts. The remaining two days would be covered by myself and Susan, filling in the gaps, including nights and weekends.

Melanie, the representative from Hell Cometh, brought Lisa to my mom's bedside. Despite our concerns about her appearance, multi-colored hair and several tattoos, we went along with Melanie's recommendation and decided to give Lisa a try. It turned out that she had just graduated from Hell Cometh's hardly adequate training program (cough!), and this was her first assignment. However, they still charged us their top tier rate of $22.50 an hour.

Lisa showed up late three of her first five days and wanted to leave early one of those. She left gastric explosions in the toilet at Mom's house that *guess who* had to clean up two evenings in a row. She also stole 80 – 100 oxycodone pills and was *unavailable* when Mom needed her. To top it all off, she was discovered sleeping on the job. She had taken so many oxycodone pills that she was incapacitated. She had done the stupid thief thing and left the empty bottles in the cabinet. Otherwise, I would not have noticed the theft so quickly.

I sent the agency some pictures of my findings and immediately requested that she be fired and replaced. However, they only moved her to another client/victim.

Hell Cometh would not do anything further unless a police report was filed. So, I had to file a formal police report for the missing opioids that Lisa had stolen. They finally fired her after she signed a full confession forty-five days later.

I also renegotiated the $22.50 per hour that was charged to $19.00 per hour, plus a $500 inconvenience fee. Can you imagine the stress of working, caring for your mom while under hospice care, and dealing with an unscrupulous agency??

Next came Annette. She arrived at Mom's at 9:45 the next morning, not at the scheduled time of 8 a.m., delaying my work schedule. Her supervisor, Sylvia, didn't arrive until an hour later, further delaying my schedule. Her excuse was that there was a mix-up about the address. It was becoming apparent that this agency had many organizational deficiencies.

Initially, Annette was very sweet and caring with Mom, and we all liked her. She performed her duties well. There was a time, I was using Hell Cometh, and then employed the other competing agency, Second Agency, for additional help. Eventually, Annette agreed to transfer to Second Agency for slightly better pay.

However, after about three months, her personal problems began to appear. She was either late or a no-show at times. She wanted to cut her agreed-upon hours and began sleeping on the job. On one of her no-show days, the agency sent another caregiver, Lexie, to replace Annette. She was so inattentive that she didn't even notice that Mom had slightly vomited on her nightgown. Lexie was busy watching TV with Mom when I came in from work, and I immediately noticed her soiled nightgown.

Annette's growing inability to stick to the schedule and some inattentiveness became more than I could handle. I chastised her one day, and she didn't return for a few days. When she did, we talked, and everything seemed back on track. She even promised that she would remain *'til the end*. However, because of yet another personal crisis, she did not. Another unfortunate sidebar to this story is that since I, the daughter, was dealing with scheduling and the agencies, my sister-in-law was unaware of many of the scheduling nightmares.

I always tried to make my and Susan's schedules fair and thought we always had good discussions regarding such. About three months into Mom's five-month journey, my sister-in-law decided I was causing the problems with Annette and I guess didn't like the schedule at times. I don't know, she wouldn't talk about it. I guess that she just came to that conclusion and that she would no longer assist me with Mom's care. This made my job even more difficult. I texted her once and asked for some relief, to which she replied, "I'll have to ask Ty," her husband, my brother. She later did help a little, but the rift never healed. During these amazingly stressful times, previous dysfunctional family issues inevitably reappeared.

I survived the caregiver trials with assistance from certain ones, especially Renee, from Second Agency, who was caring for Mom on her days away from caring for Dad. She turned out to be the best caregiver. During the last forty-five days, the care was mostly split among Renee, myself, and another caregiver.

Mom was slowly growing weaker with time passing as her vital organs were being clogged with cancerous growth and shutting down. Beginning this odyssey, we tried to get her up some and take her around the house in a wheelchair. But that became increasingly more difficult. The only time during this entire five-month ordeal I ever saw her cry was when we wheeled her outside one day, and it became overwhelmingly apparent to her that she would never take care of her yard and return to normal again—a sad moment.

During all of this time with caregivers, hospice nurses were visiting Mom twice a week. They administered pain medications, filled out their reports, and took care of any other medical-related needs. Generally, they were good at their job, but they were only as good as their communication from the patient and the caregivers.

When each nurse arrived, they always asked Mom how she was doing. She would light up, smile, and say, "Just fine." There was a nasty situation that happened when she became severely constipated, and we learned the caregivers were not recording her lack of bowel movements. (Seems common, huh?) This happened on a day when the hospice nurses couldn't come. So, I called a retired nurse friend of mine, and we proceeded to dig feces out of Mom's failing body. Even though caregivers, hospice nurses, and others were part of the scenario, the importance of responsible family members to take up the slack and notice the *misses* cannot be overstated. *It is a very lonely and stressful job for involved family members.*

As time slowly marched on, Mom's condition worsened, and the hospice nurses came more often, more closely monitoring her pain. There were some brighter moments in those days, however. One of the hospice nurses was a very accomplished bluegrass fiddler. One Sunday morning, she, a couple of her church musicians, and a good friend of ours brought their guitars and fiddles and played and sang for her until Sunday lunchtime.

Another bright spot was that she didn't lose her appetite until the last two months. She enjoyed friends and family bringing her food. One of her favorites was fried apple pies from a local diner. She also enjoyed watermelon that I cut into pieces as small as my little fingernail and fed her. It was cool, moist, and easy to chew. Point made here; I told one of the caregivers that she liked watermelon. When I got to her house that evening, I cut up a watermelon. I can still hear her voice, "Oh, that tastes so good." Either the caregiver didn't try to give her small bites of watermelon or gave her something else she could not easily chew.

During all of this time of taking care of her, there were many problems we had to endure. In the beginning, there was the caregiver agency. We found that their administration was somewhat unresponsive and that they did not carefully screen their employees. The pay scale in that industry is so low that, frequently, low-quality people are placed in charge of caring for their loved ones. I spent many hours negotiating with and complaining to agency administrators in an attempt to get better care for my mother. *You must be proactive*!

Also, during the five months leading up to her death, she continually avoided discussing the aftermath. Do you have a will, a trust, a personal representative? What special items do you want to go to whom? Unfortunately, few people want to face their mortality. They are frequently very reluctant to share these things with family members. Hey! We don't get outta here alive!

Mom did have a will, a trust, and powers of attorney in place, but she wouldn't let me or my brother look at her documents. Wouldn't it have been better if the entire immediate family was gathered together for a meeting to discuss the aftermath? Well, that didn't happen, and she passed away in August. In the days that followed, we then reviewed her will and trust.

Everything was, as we suspected, to be split equally between myself and my brother. However, the one sheet listing her assets and accounts was BLANK. We had no idea how many accounts she had or where they were. We ended up on a wild goose chase of watching her mail every day for statements, keeping her online account active while looking through mounds of papers.

We thought we had found all of her bank statements until I found a tub of old papers one day. I took them home to my husband, and he went through them. He found an out-of-town account at a credit union containing thousands of dollars. We were shocked and saddened that there was never communication regarding her assets. This lack of communication led to family members' misconceptions concerning problem-solving during the illness and creating rifts that have never healed.

Finally, a word about hospice and our legally hamstrung medical system: hospice does a good job of helping one die with less pain. However, they and all our medical systems have become rather impersonal. They spend so much time filling out reports that they actually spend very little time just looking at the patient as a human being and exploring their emotional needs. The result? A lack of communication and impaired care. They frequently don't get to the bottom of their patient's specific needs and problems. The moral of this and every story involving a dying family member—*As a family member and caregiver, you must remain proactive!*

Chapter 3

Stubborn Behavior Outweighs Logic

Cathy works in the tech industry and has a very good job with huge responsibility and a good income. Her kids are grown and out of the house, and she has a good husband. Her dad, Carl, lives three hours away on the family farm. Carl is on Medicaid, and that pays for part-time home health care. Carl hired Emily through an agency. Emily worked four hours a day, four days a week.

One day, Cathy spent $200 on groceries to bring to her dad. When she arrived, she opened the refrigerator door to put away the groceries. She noticed three different kinds of coffee creamers. "That's odd!" she thought. "Dad drinks his coffee black!" She questioned Carl, and he replied, "It's Emily's." Of course, this means nothing by itself, but it is a small thing speaking to the familiar and comfortable relationship that seemed to be developing between them, at least in Carl's mind.

She made another trip to visit her dad a couple of months later. The living room looked ok, but she started looking around in his bedroom and the other rooms. There were cobwebs in the corners and dust everywhere. The cobwebs had been there so long that they were even coated with dust!

Emily was there, and Cathy asked Emily about cleaning the other rooms. Emily replied that she didn't work for Cathy. Cathy looked at her dad, then Carl said, "Well, honey, if you don't mind, it would be nice to have the rooms cleaned up a little." Emily then proceeded only to pick up a few things off the floor. After some time, Cathy commented to her dad, saying that she really didn't see Emily doing a lot around the house. Well, Carl admitted that he knew that, but she does just enough, and they enjoy watching TV together. He told Cathy that he was *in love* with Emily. Cathy replied, "Daddy, you might be in love with her, but I promise you, she wouldn't be here if she wasn't getting paid!"

One day, Cathy called her dad. Carl said Emily had quit because her back was hurting from doing work around the house. Emily hadn't been there for three days. Cathy asked her dad if he'd like to stay with her for a week. He seemed pretty agreeable to that. Two days later, she called him, getting ready to drive three hours to pick him up from his home. Carl told Cathy, "Nope. Emily returned." Cathy said, "What do you mean, she returned?" Carl replied, "Well, she needs the money, so I'm going to stay here. Everything's fine." Cathy relayed to me, "You know that agency still got paid by Medicaid even though she didn't work last week! That agency didn't bother to stop the payments for one week." So, Carl, her dad, placed Emily, the "*ScareTaker*" ahead of being with his daughter.

A few months later, Medicaid rules changed, and the agency reviewed his situation. They decided to remove his state-funded caregiver because Carl met ADL (Activities of Daily Living) guidelines. Of course, Carl found out about Emily's true love for him. She vanished, as happens in every case. Carl called Emily many times and even had a friend take him to her house. She wouldn't even answer the door.

Cathy decided to appeal Medicaid's decision, and a court date was scheduled. She drove three hours for the event, including videoing Carl and his abilities at an agency-approved location. Carl could feed himself and go to the bathroom, with his walker, alone. However, he is legally blind and cannot see well enough to prepare a meal. He can make sandwiches or eat beanie weenies but not cook a meal. He is confused enough that he can't sequence the necessary steps in meal preparation. His mobility is extremely impaired, but he can manage to move very slowly through the few rooms of his small house with a walker or cane. The end result? The court denied Cathy's appeal, and Carl was left without a caregiver.

He has been left in the care of his drug-addicted grandson, Shane, when he is not in jail. Shane is 42 years old and a career criminal. Cathy's sister can rarely help because Carl thinks she is mean, lazy, and doesn't want her around.

Cathy visited her dad one weekend and noticed three shoeboxes of jewelry. She questioned Shane about the shoeboxes. He replied that he had stolen them from caregivers who had stolen jewelry from senior women they had cared for! Shane was cutting the jewelry into pieces and categorizing the stones from the jewelry settings. *Thieves know thieves, druggies know druggies.*

Cathy, the responsible daughter, has been left to manage his care even though she lives three hours away and works full time. Anyone who has ever taken care of an aging person understands the stress, responsibility, and difficulty.

On numerous occasions, Cathy has asked her dad why he didn't go and live in a local assisted living facility. He knows people there, and he would get daily meals and not be burdened by his grandson. His response has been, "Shane wouldn't have a place to live," or "what would I do with all my stuff?"

Having his drug-addicted grandson around is better than being at home alone. Shane verbally and physically abuses his grandfather. He found Shane lying in a ditch one evening. He stopped, woke him up, and attempted to put him in the car. The drug-addicted Shane broke off the car's rearview mirror and hit his grandfather in the head with it, causing profuse bleeding.

After they arrived home, Carl locked himself in the bedroom and called 911. The local sheriff arrested Shane. Then, on the day of court, Carl dropped the charges. His fear of being alone outweighed his fear of Shane. It is unbelievable but true that he would rather live in a drug-infested, filthy home with abuse rather than be alone or at a care facility where he knows people.

Cathy eventually found a woman nearby that she paid $10 per hour for six hours on one day to prepare meals for the week, do some cleaning and laundry. However, she had to quit after a month to care for her family.

Cathy has called The Department of Human Services (DHS), the prosecuting attorney's office, and the Attorney General's office, but did not receive help.

Shane was arrested again recently. Carl doesn't know what to do. He doesn't want to be told what to do by Cathy. He knows he cannot remain in his house by himself, but he doesn't want to even try an assisted living facility for two weeks. Cathy is at the point of giving up. Instead of daily calls, she now talks to him once a week. She, like some of us, has learned that she just can't care as much. Parents might make the "adult child" their healthcare POA, but then, what's the point? Carl doesn't care to listen to reason. It remains, as of this writing, a very heartrending and difficult situation.

Chapter 4

Hoochie Momma

Ben was 84 and widowed. His son worked nearby and had a good reputation in the community. However, as sometimes is the case, he and his son did not get along and were estranged. Ben realized he was aging rather profoundly and decided, on his own, that he needed some help.

He hired a woman he knew, Brenda, to become a caregiver. She was a rather attractive woman in her early fifties. She brought with her two friends to help but appointed herself as the lead caregiver for this aging man. She came to work wearing scant clothing that exposed enough of her large breasts to make the old man notice. On warm days, she'd show up in short shorts.

Well, Ben, like many, really enjoyed the view and her attention. Brenda and Ben began running around while she was on duty as if they were a married couple. She began spending Ben's money, at first for excessive groceries and then other special things for herself. Now, old Ben was having fun with his fantasy relationship, and he liked to party a little, so they began visiting a local casino. They ate and drank and spent lots of money on the gambling machines.

On days off, when either of the other two caregivers were on duty, Ben would stay at home watching them clean his house and attend to his needs. After a while, these two became unhappy that they were doing all the work and having none of the fun, so a conflict arose.

So, this lecherous woman, Brenda, whom Ben had hired, called a home health agency to replace her friends who had quit. The home health agency supplied two women to help with house cleaning and chores when Brenda was not there.

Ben had fallen head over heels for Brenda and would watch the clock for her to get off her other parttime job. He began calling her continuously during the time she was not on duty. Although she rarely answered his calls, this small rejection did nothing to deter Ben.

"Hoochie Mamma," as the agency staff later called her, took over Ben's care and his mind. It is fairly easy to guess where this story is going. The casino trips and the partying continued. Ben was losing his nest egg at a record pace. In that one year, he lost over $20,000 just at the casino and restaurants!

"Hoochie Mamma," for his upcoming 85th birthday, even took him to a striptease club and paid for a lap dancer, with Ben's money. Soon, Ben's resources were exhausted. He could no longer pay "Hoochie Mamma" and the agency. The agency withdrew their two caregivers, and, since the party was over, "Hoochie Mamma" disappeared faster than a speeding bullet.

Ben, now alone, became extremely depressed and began wandering around his neighborhood looking disheveled and downtrodden. Neighbors noticed and called his estranged son. His dad was now destitute and helpless. His son was forced to place Ben under the umbrella of the state's Medicaid.

Where is poor old Ben now? He was removed from his home and is now living in a subpar nursing home being paid for by Medicaid. Well, yes, as in this case and many others, it *is* his money, and he can do what he wants to with it. This is what can happen when a family member or trusted loved one is not involved in the home health care decisions!

Chapter 5

Who Can You Trust?

As we find ourselves moving into a new position in our family in the middle generation, we are thrust into new caregiving roles. Raising a family is a learning experience in the needs of children and adolescents. Caring for our elderly relatives, especially parents, challenges us from many, often unexpected aspects.

I cared for my aging mother as she moved into a world of dementia, but we were fortunate to have an assisted living provider who cared for her with my limited help. Just the stress of knowing she had to rely on other people constantly further triggered her paranoia that someone was taking her money. Sadly, her dementia was the culprit that caused her to forget where she hid it. I admit that I was also a bit paranoid until I started finding some of the hiding places. She never had a personal caregiver just for her.

It is important to realize that when our loved ones are in others' care, we naturally feel anxious and may have difficulty trusting caregivers. I learned to trust my mother's care at her assisted living residence after witnessing four years of their care.

With such a positive experience with caregivers, I stepped in to care for my deceased husband's stepmother, Ann, with a positive outlook and good expectations. Due to a chronic back problem, she became unable to walk her dog, Cici, while living in an independent living community, and I could not meet all of her frequent needs. We searched for someone to help walk Cici. We tried a few unsuccessfully before a friend of mine, Milly, offered. We were so happy to have someone I knew that we felt we could depend on.

Milly was eager to walk Cici twice a day at the times requested and immediately bonded with her. This arrangement worked very well for several months until Milly decided she couldn't do it any longer. Milly said the money wasn't worth her time, even though she had talked Ann into paying for gas and had added hours by offering to shop for her. She offered to do more and to stay longer, but Ann did not want more help. After all, Ann had me take her places and shop for her, and her community included cleaning and meals. She was still pretty able to take care of herself on normal days with little assistance. I made trips more often to fill in with walking Cici until Ann could go walking again.

About a year later, Ann fell and broke her arm and shoulder. She had a neighbor who had hired some dependable caregivers in the past that she recommended. We had a rotation of very pleasant and hardworking ladies who came to her home to care for her and Cici. They worked out well for a while until one of them hurt her back and could not work and the other one quit.

Milly eventually heard about our situation and inquired about helping out. Ann was eager to hire her again, even though she was disappointed when Milly had left us stranded a year earlier when she quit. I admit I was relieved to have a replacement that she liked.

I checked out in-home agencies, but the expense was so much that Ann wanted to try referred caregivers, like Milly. I was a little torn because Milly didn't charge much less than an agency, but it appeared it could work well. She was so sweet and constantly offering to do more and more to help.

Ann started becoming friends with Milly as Milly poured out her heart about her family and all of her problems. She especially spoke about her financial problems she had and how bad her car was. You couldn't help but feel sorry for her.

Chapter 5: Who Can You Trust?

One day, on a planned trip to buy groceries, Milly showed up a little late because of car trouble. Ann offered to let her drive her car to take them to the store. Milly loved it and talked and talked about how great it was and how she wished she could afford a better car. This became the first of many trips to the store in this better car.

Before long, Ann said she was planning to donate her car to Kars for Kids when she couldn't drive anymore but told me maybe she should offer it to Milly, who needed it. I found that very generous and thoughtful until I remembered that Milly was married, and they also had a truck. I had also noticed that Milly had changed her hours. She was originally asked to work from 7 a.m. to 11 a.m., so the first dog walk would be when they usually rose for the day. With no explanation, she requested to move from 8 a.m. to noon. Ann normally ate lunch at 11:30 a.m., so it was natural to offer Milly lunch, which she eagerly accepted, *every single time.*

Often lunch also occurred when they were out shopping or leaving a doctor's visit or some other errand, nothing to be suspicious about. Or was it? I noticed more and more little favors Milly took advantage of... nothing big or drawing great attention.

Before I knew it, Ann had agreed to give Milly her car. I felt very uneasy about it and spoke with her, suggesting she sell it to Milly for a low price rather than give it away. She agreed that selling was a better idea. We felt Milly needed to contribute something. I told Milly she could have the car for what she could sell her car for. Her car was worth about a third of this car's value. This car was an older Cadillac with only 30,000 miles on it. She told me what her mechanic estimated she could get for her car.

While Ann was recovering from the arm breaks, she suddenly had a catastrophe with insulin and wound up in the hospital. Because she was so weak and getting confused, I enlisted a professional caregiver service around the clock. Milly was not pleased that others were helping and that they seemed to be well received. Milly came to visit her in the hospital and started asking about the car. I asked Milly to please stop talking about the car. We had agreed to sell it to her at a great price, much to her advantage. The thought of Ann not being able to drive again was depressing her, and I didn't want it to be discussed so much.

I had to leave the hospital room, and when I returned, Milly was huddled at Ann's side whispering. I overheard her complaining about how much it would cost to fix her car to get the amount she could sell it for. I was not happy. I again approached her and asked her to please stop talking about the car. She was going to get it and didn't need to keep pressing the issue. She was getting a super good deal.

Additionally, I had very generously offered to pay in advance for the coming month what Milly would have made working for us, so she had money to pay to fix her car that she was selling. My condition was that she would take Ann's laundry and pick up necessities, and she would help me move her. Ann became so ill that I was told I had to move her to assisted living, and she couldn't go home. I knew I would need help to make that happen even though I knew a good mover that would pack and help set up her new apartment.

I had asked Milly to visit Ann at the hospital, getting laundry while there, and meet me to pick up Cici that she said she wanted to adopt. Instead of visiting Ann, she went shopping for herself and met me to get Cici. I wound up having to take the laundry. That was the time that I had prepaid her for the month that she blew off. This was just more of the signs of taking advantage of a weak person. She had convinced us she was a friend, *a trustworthy friend.*

Magically, she got exactly what the mechanic said the car would sell for. The next week, I arranged to meet her at the Department of Motor Vehicles to transfer the title and registration. It wasn't until the clerk asked the selling price that she told me how much she got for the car she sold.... The price now on the one she was buying. When the clerk told her how much it cost to register, she looked at me as though she thought I was paying. I looked away and started walking off. She paid.

Chapter 5: Who Can You Trust?

Milly was supposed to give me cash for the car, but as we left, the clerk told me she hadn't gotten the money yet, but it was at her bank. So, I told her I would take her by the bank on the way to Ann's house to get the car. She got her money when I stopped at the bank, but I wondered how long she would have waited had I not insisted that we stop there to get it.

Once Ann was moved to assisted living, I hired professional caregivers full time, and Milly was no longer needed or wanted. As the move was happening, I had asked Milly to get some things not yet removed from the house. She insisted she needed to take the caregiver that was with us that day. When they returned, the caregiver shared they had gone through the house to look around because there would be a yard sale. Milly also noticed a bag of batteries and said her husband could use them.

I told her we were planning an estate sale and not a yard sale. I was then a bit nervous that the things Ann had were being shared with someone she didn't even know. Trust was eroding more and more all the time.

After Ann was settled, we maintained professional caregiving services fulltime to care for her. Milly had Cici that was now hers. Instead of just going away as I asked her to, she kept calling Ann and talking about the car and Cici.

She even showed up with Cici one day and asked the caregiver to walk Cici so she could visit! I couldn't believe that when I heard it. I again asked her to please leave Ann alone. Seeing Cici and talking with Milly kept emotions high. She was trying to adjust to her new situation.

Milly finally told me she would just talk to Ann and didn't have to listen to me, even though I was the one managing everything. Ann had gotten so weak and didn't need to be more upset, although she still had me pay for any care of Cici. The only thing that kept Milly away finally was the pandemic. Even at that, she would call and wind up asking for money for dog food, vet, or whatever.

Ann passed away that fall. I had blocked Milly from communicating with me when she told me she wouldn't talk to me, so I didn't contact her. I knew she would learn of Ann's passing. She contacted my daughter to tell her how mean I was for not telling her. I didn't tell her, but I gave the vet $500 for future dog care, even though it had been hers for a year already.

I find it very difficult to know how to deal with people in your home caring for the seniors. I trusted the professional caregivers more because they did background checks and had strict procedures that made them professional with the agency I hired. I'm sure a bad apple could slip through, but I think they provided very good people and dealt with problem employees efficiently.

They had rules like don't take food or money from your patient. Don't talk about your problems and make them feel like they have to take care of you. Shift every conversation to focus on the patient, lending your experiences to shed light on theirs. You can become close without becoming like family. At least with a company, you don't have to manage the people personally. You talk to their manager and let them deal with problems. You are so vulnerable you have to protect yourself and your family as best you can.

Chapter 6

The Useless Caregiver

My husband, Grant, was diagnosed with esophageal cancer. Upon this devastating news, he first went to our local oncologists. The doctors confirmed that current treatments might slow down the progression of the disease but not ultimately change the outcome. Like most victims of this horrible diagnosis, he decided to pursue the best available treatments. For two years, we frequently traveled to MD Anderson. Well, as one doctor had commented, of course, there is not a cure for cancer.

During his treatments, he did have some pleasant responses and was able to continue his good life. We continued our Friday evening get-togethers with friends and even traveled some. However, the disease did progress, and our goal became intensely focused on managing daily living.

Eventually, cancer had spread to his liver, and I knew from his hospital tests and his spitting up blood that he only had one to two, possibly, days left here on earth. He was sent home from the hospital to begin hospice care.

Hospice referred us to a home care agency. I naively assumed this referred agency's caregivers were Certified Nursing Assistants. The owner of the agency, Leigh, met Grant and me at home. She interviewed us, and when I walked outside with her as she was leaving, she voiced her opinion that Grant would probably be with us for a couple of weeks. Had she been taking care of Grant for over two years?

I knew the stages he was going through and where he was in his disease when we got home from the hospital the day before he perished. Leigh, didn't! I was very surprised at this since I had been with my mother when she passed and a few others. So, I knew "the signs." Leigh said she would have someone come to our house in a few hours.

I called Grant's adult children and told them to come over and stay the night if they liked since I felt he might be in his final hours. The home health caregiver, Michelle, arrived at 6 p.m. I assumed she was in the nursing field, considering that Leigh knew Grant's circumstance. She should have sent at least a CNA or an LPN who could have been some help! We sat together with Grant. I thought she would be knowledgeable and informative. With Grant in his final hours, she sat there, suggesting that maybe we should get him jello, or maybe we should get him a cola or just this and that. She had little to offer.

When Grant's children arrived, we moved him into the hospital bed in the back bedroom. He had been such a tall, strong man just a few years ago and had a booming voice. Now, he was just skin and bones and had shrunk so much.

I remained near Grant throughout the night, monitoring his breathing. It was becoming more and more shallow. The children remained in the living area, sleeping on the couch and chairs. Michelle, the "Scare-Taker," had gone to sleep in a spare bedroom. I thought she, of all people, would be close by and attentive to Grant!? I awakened his children when I could barely hear Grant's breathing and told them we need to tell him goodbye. I had administered so much morphine to him earlier and knew he would not last much longer. After we had said our final goodbyes, I checked his vital signs then pronounced Grant's passing at 4:50 a.m.

I called hospice and the coroner's office. Michelle, the *nurse's aide*, as I had referred her as, remained asleep until she heard all of us talking. She woke up at 5:45 a.m. and asked what was going on. I told her Grant had passed and she could leave. She was zero help.

Chapter 6: The Useless Caregiver

You couldn't believe my astonishment when I received a bill in the mail for $276 from the agency a few weeks later! I called the agency and let them know that I would not be paying that amount, and they'd be lucky to get $100! I didn't need someone to show up and then go to bed while my husband was dying!

Chapter 7

Friend or Foe

Mom was diagnosed with a rare disease and was given six years to live at the age of 54. She and Daddy immediately made an appointment for a second opinion. The second opinion suggested that she had type A Parkinson's Disease. Later on, it was confirmed that the first diagnosis was correct, corticobasal degeneration, a very rare form of Parkinson's. This is a progressive neurological disorder characterized by cell loss and deterioration of specific areas of the brain. Affected individuals often initially experience motor abnormalities in one limb that eventually spreads to affect all the arms and legs. Daddy told me all this after her tragic death.

During Mom's illness, we hired caregivers privately, depending upon recommendations from friends and acquaintances. The first one, Jenny, was my ex-husband's girlfriend at the time. She needed a job, so my daughter and ex-husband introduced her to Mom. They encouraged Mom to hire her. She was supposed to help her walk to the bathroom, cook her meals, and take care of other basic needs. At that time, Mom could still get around with a walker. Initially, Jenny did a good job but soon began showing up for work drunk and seemingly on some kind of illicit drugs.

I lived a few hours away, and I couldn't quickly intervene. I called Mom daily, so I could find out if Jenny had shown up. Then I could decide if Mom needed immediate attention. Jenny was often late, or sometimes even a no-show, so Mom went without food or water for extended periods.

Whether she came late or left early, she was mostly sitting with Mother, telling her all her problems and using her as a counselor rather than caring for her needs. Daddy was a nurse anesthesiologist and worked long hours at the hospital. My brother, who was unemployed at the time, would occasionally pitch in and help fill in the gaps as a part-time family caregiver. My sister lived far away in the Northeast, so it was very difficult for us to monitor the situation in a hands-on way. Other caregivers came and went, but mostly, they were just like Jenny, wrought with problems and frequently substance abusers.

Soon, Mom reached the point where she needed help in the evenings as well, and Daddy was working more and more, so she spent way too much time alone, unable to help herself. Daddy would change her and dress her in the morning before he left for the hospital. Also, he would wheel her into the living room, set up her drink, turn on the television, and sit for two to three hours waiting for her caregiver to arrive.

Erika was the next caregiver after Jenny. She usually showed up late but was a real charmer, an accomplished con artist. She stole from my parents, but her charm completely fooled them. Unfortunately, when one's need is intense, good judgment frequently becomes happenstance. She knew how to manipulate Daddy and my brother so that they did not see her fraudulent intent.

Unfortunately, Daddy became ill later. He was diagnosed with leukemia not long after Mom became ill. Erika would rub his feet and charm him while Mother was unable to enter into the happenings. Family heirlooms, clothing, and money came up missing. After Mom's diamond earrings disappeared, Mom desperately grabbed my hand, and though she could hardly speak by then, she managed to eke out, "Get her out of here!" She couldn't tell me why, but we knew the situation was way out of control.

We were all overwhelmed with the entire state of their lives. We all just began praying to God that we had to have divine help, and, you know what, help came. Erika left, and an angel appeared. My parents, both nurses, had spent their lives taking care of each other and deserved better than a fraudster.

A new caregiver, Kathy, arrived. She took care of Mom with all her heart and soul, and that saved the day. To this day, on some level, I worry that I should have dropped everything and moved to my parent's home and become their caregiver. However, it would have meant that my children would have had no mother present and that Daddy would have had to support me. In other words, he would have had more mouths to feed. I think my situation is not uncommon today, and it is unfortunate that being elderly and ill comes with so much insidious intent and maltreatment.

Chapter 8

Care from Afar

Mom was sharp to the day of her death. She passed 51 weeks before Dad died. She had hired caregivers that had helped them for years. To this day, I have no idea if they were independents or from an agency. Our parents lived in Texas, and we lived in California. When we were in Texas during Mom's hospice, I heard Dad repeat stories and made a mental note that he may need further evaluation once Mom's needs were met. Mom, wanting control beyond the grave, insisted on being informed about what we would do with Dad. In hindsight, that made more sense than we knew at the time.

One day, I noticed through Dad's opened shirt that his chest was yellow. No caregiver or visiting nurse had noticed, and Dad just shrugged it off when I mentioned it. I had him call his doctor. He was like a child balking and complaining, but he did call. Then he told the nurse on the phone, in a whining voice, that his daughter was making him call. The doctor wanted to see him. It was serious jaundice, which pointed to potential organ failure. He was taken to the hospital and was there when Mom passed.

By that time, all of us had returned to our lives with Mom's impending death hanging over us. I got the call in the middle of the night from the caregiver that Mom was dying. I called my siblings to call her and tell her goodbye. I had just spoken to her the day before when my son got married. I figured I could call last. But my brother seemed to avoid wanting to call and kept insisting that I call Mom next. Arguing was wasting time we didn't have, so I called her and was the last to speak with her before she passed. She couldn't talk anymore, and I don't know how much she heard.

Dad was returned home when he was better. I don't think we truly understood how bad Dad was. Mom, to the end, kept silent about Dad's condition. My sister called him and told him to get things ready because she was moving him to her home in California as soon as she could arrange it, in a few months. In the meantime, he told the caregivers to take whatever they wanted. They tore things from the walls and even took an antique trundle bed. We will never know what all they took. All Dad could tell us is that he didn't mean for them to do that.

During his time before my sister went to get him, he had also taken the caregivers out for meals quite often. To be fair, he may have wanted to do that, or he may have been manipulated, which wouldn't have been hard to do after he had lost his life's companion. In the end, I think they took advantage of a man with dementia, poor mobility, and a need for company. Mom had kept them in line. Dad was a pushover, and we were in another state. Better communication with Mom and the caregivers could have led to a better outcome.

Linda Mac Dougall, M.A., HHP, CMT, is the author of the ultimate guide to working in the senior care arena, "The SPIRIT Method of Massage for Seniors: Raising the Bar…A Primer for Massage Therapists and Caregivers". After decades of working with people with developmental disabilities, she now works with seniors as she has become one herself. Today, she lives in Southern California with her toy poodle. www.loveyourlongevity.com

Chapter 9

The Trusted Caregiver

My parents were a typical 1950's couple who married young, spent time in the army, moved to a bedroom community outside of a large city, and settled down to a full life from the 1960s through the 2010s. Dad worked hard, Mom was supportive, and they were very active in both their church and community.

By 2013, however, as Dad entered his 80s, mild dementia was beginning to creep in. We noticed when he would drive out to get doughnuts on a Sunday morning and take much longer than he should have. He was loath to admit it, but he would get lost. So, in the early summer of that year, they contacted a home health care agency, and a caregiver, Maria, was sent. Maria was a sweet, diminutive person who was always on top of things and ready to jump in and help. Originally from Mexico, she had an older husband and a teenage son. She was in her early 40s.

Maria would arrive at my parent's house around 8:00 a.m. each morning and leave around 4:00 p.m. each afternoon throughout the week. She was mainly there to help Dad, but Mother benefited from her care as well, if anything, due to no longer having the stress of looking after Dad alone.

Toward the end of 2013, my parents started thinking about moving to an assisted living facility, as Dad's memory was becoming thinner and thinner. Had Maria not been around to help, they would have surely moved in much sooner. So for the next two and a half years, Maria became part of the family. She was always dependable. She would go on small outings with us, like to the Texas State Fair. She was everything you wanted a caregiver to be: helpful, dependable, and almost invisible.

It's my opinion that this is what allowed my parents to be *taken* because they trusted and, frankly, loved Maria. She was such a godsend to them that my generous parents would naturally oblige if she needed something. Unlike my sister, I'm not convinced that Maria was plotting and planning on cheating my parents. Perhaps it began innocently and developed into her way of getting extra pay for extra work. Below are examples of how we found my parents had helped her, most of which we did not find out about until much after the fact when we started going through my parent's checkbook and financials after we found out about the big *financial gift* my parents gave.

At some time, they were discussing Maria's son and how he would be a senior in high school soon. Maria said something to my mother about how she was sad that neither she nor her husband could afford to get him a cherished *senior ring*. Whether she planted that seed on purpose or not, it worked, and Mom agreed to chip in and help out. Later, it seems like her son wanted to go on a short *exchange trip* overseas with his school. Mom paid for the trip. We only found out about this when my sister found a thank you note that Maria's son had written.

Maria apologized for being late one time, saying she was nervous because her car tires were so worn. Mom and Dad bought her four new tires. Maria broke a tooth but didn't have dental insurance or the means to pay for it. Mom paid her dental bill. Maria had foot surgery at one point, and my sister flew down to help take care of my dad since Maria would be out of commission for a week or two. We found out later that my mother had paid for her surgery.

I received a call from my mother, saying her accountant was there and was basically making her call me and explain something to me. "Bill said I have to let you know about the money I'm giving Maria because

Chapter 9: The Trusted Caregiver

you or the trust will probably have to pay taxes on it at the end of the year, and he didn't want this to be a surprise." "Ok," I asked, "how much?" My mother answered, "Forty thousand dollars."

It seems that Maria (who divorced her husband and found a new boyfriend while in service with my parents) needed the money to give to her boyfriend. His wife in Mexico would not give him a divorce so that he and Maria could get married. He was hoping that by giving her some money, she would agree to a divorce and Maria and he could have their wedding. So, they brought this plan to Mother, who would have kept it secret from us if it were not for my parents' accountant. This made me really angry, so I looked up the rules and guidelines for healthcare workers on the home health care agency's website. It was very clear that their workers were not to ask for money and should not have even hinted at needing some sort of help, even if just in passing. Maria had clearly violated the terms, and once my sister let the organization know, they fired her in October 2015.

The fact that my sister reported her to her employer really infuriated my mother, who threatened to cut my sister out of the will and canceled an upcoming trip to visit her. The events, as you see, leading up to her dismissal had become much more egregious.

This all happened during my parents' move into a senior living center. Even after they moved, Maria had still been going over to visit my dad in the Memory Care Unit. My parents were very sad to see Maria go, as she truly had felt like one of the family. But, ultimately, they were wise enough to know it was the right thing to do, and fortunately, at this point, they both lived in the senior center and were well attended to by staff.

Shortly after this happened, as mentioned earlier, my sister started pouring through Mother's checkbook. There was a check written to Maria here for $1,000 and there for $1,500, etc. Mom claimed she would write the checks, which Maria would cash and then use that money to buy groceries. Mom never asked for receipts or double-checked to see if everything was adding up. Clearly, Maria had found a means of pocketing a little extra money each month, in addition to the other gifts my parents were giving her.

We found out later that Maria and Jose never gave his wife the money but would most likely use it to purchase a small piece of land in Mexico. We'll never know for sure because Maria and her family vanished soon after being fired.

– by Tom R.

Chapter 10

DHS Removed Her

Dianne was 93 years of age and had lived alone for thirty years. She divorced her husband when she was in her early sixties. Her three sons had moved to different states establishing their own independent lives and families. They occasionally checked in with their mom. In this story, it is important to understand that this was a military family and that the dad, the authoritative head of the household, was the stereotypical military officer. He was accustomed to dealing with most, including his sons, in a rather regimented way. The family disconnect that this created carried over into all family dynamics, even after his death.

Having been an old friend of the oldest son and a realtor, I was asked to prepare the home for sale and place it on the market. However, trust and past reliance upon each other was lacking, so I was placed into this difficult situation as an outsider, attempting to create new dynamics that might allow progress and order in the final days of this family's ordeal concerning their mother and the liquidation of her assets. She had become accustomed to relying upon her independence, beginning many years before her old age, carried over into her dealings with her sons. She would not allow them to have the tools to help her, believing that she could handle things herself and not involve them, despite their attempts to become involved. Consequently, when she really needed help, they were somewhat reticent to act immediately. The details of that disconnect are as follows.

I received a call from Mark, her oldest son, in late April. He was very distraught and told me that the Department of Human Services (DHS) had removed his mom from her home!? It had taken DHS about three hours to remove her, and she was now in a mental facility. How did this happen? Dianne's caregiver, Becky, had been caring for her a few hours each day for the past three years. It seemed like a good relationship. Mark and his younger brother Bryan had met Becky when they visited their mom each year.

Becky told Dianne that she needed to leave because her husband had become ill and needed to relocate. Dianne was upset by this news but began calling a few home health care agencies to find a replacement. Becky had been hired independently rather than through an agency, so her fees were almost half of what home health care agencies typically charge. Dianne told Becky to contact her son Mark and let him know she was leaving and that Dianne needed some help. Becky never made that call because she and Dianne had gotten into an argument about some items missing from her home, and Dianne wanted some of the other things she had given Becky returned. Becky stormed out, and a couple of days later, called the Department of Human Services.

Becky reported an elderly lady was living by herself and unable to care for herself, that she was disheveled in appearance and somewhat incapacitated. Ms. Smith, an officer with DHS, called Mark and told him that he needed to get someone to care for his mom. Mark could not do that instantly since he lived out of state and would need a few days to find help for his mother. Mark called his mother, and she assured Mark she was fine, and she was looking for someone.

The next morning, Dianne heard a knock on the door. When she opened the door, she faced Ms. Smith, who was a large woman with colored hair and tattoos, a police officer, and two other people who all demanded to be let in, so Dianne complied. Ms. Smith had texted Mark that she would stop by to assess his mother, to which he replied, ok. Later that same afternoon, Mark received a text saying that his mom had been removed from her home and taken to a mental facility for evaluation.

Chapter 10: DHS Removed Her

What is important to understand is that DHS, during their assessment, never called Mark and tell him that the agency intended to remove his mother from her home. Only later that afternoon was he notified by text message that the DHS removed her and took her to a mental evaluation facility. Of course, by then, it was after hours, and Mark was unable to contact Ms. Smith until the next morning.

I told Mark to call his mother's estate planning attorney, Attorney Shope, who, a year earlier, had prepared a durable power of attorney for her. However, Shope said she didn't handle these cases and referred him to another attorney who didn't return his call. After a few more phone calls, he finally found an attorney who would handle this case. Due to work and family responsibilities, the three sons couldn't travel to their mother's needs for three weeks. The youngest son, Steve, was designated as his mother's guardian and had durable power of attorney, so even if Mark or Bryan could have returned sooner, they didn't have decision-making power regarding her legal case. After the mental evaluation, Dianne was deemed incompetent, and DHS placed her in a subpar nursing home.

Mark mailed me a key to Dianne's home a week before they planned to arrive for the future court hearing. I stopped by and picked up a few things I thought she might like. A neighbor had been getting her mail and placing it on the table. There were piles and piles of magazines and junk mail related to sweepstakes and charities. I spent two hours sorting that from the necessary bills that needed to be paid. Junk mail was 95% of the total and weighed twenty pounds! There needs to be a concentrated effort to remove one's name from mailing lists to avoid getting solicitations, sweepstake offers, and scams! I took pictures of the bills and sent them to Mark, so he had account numbers, phone numbers, and amounts due. There would be substantial deposits to reconnect the utilities if they were turned off. The utility bills had not been set up as automatic drafts and were past due. Luckily, he handled those just in time.

I noticed a notebook from a home health care agency, an envelope from a local senior resource center that offered in-home care, and some phone numbers of agencies that she had written down. This particular home health care agency had left her voice mail messages that her sons heard later. Dianne had been in the process of trying to find help. She just hadn't made a decision. After going through the mail, I went to see Dianne in the nursing home. Mark had told her I would be working on selling her house later, and the sons designated me to be the local representative that the family needed for the court system. Mark and I had dated some forty years earlier and had occasionally stayed in touch.

When I walked in to see Dianne, even though I hadn't seen her in forty years, she immediately knew who I was and was very happy to see me!!? I'm using a question mark because I was startled that she knew exactly who I was! I brought her a radio she had recently purchased and a small teddy bear that I had found on her bed. She was very excited to see these items, something of familiarity. She then told me about some clothing she wanted from her closet, a certain kind of cream for her itchy legs, her hearing aids, and she mentioned her DVD player. I told her I would look for them tomorrow and see her again. I returned to my car and just cried for a minute. Why was I crying? My God! This woman is more cognizant and competent than I imagined! She doesn't belong in there! How sad! This is quite a mess!!

The next day, I went to her house, retrieved the DVD player, some clothes, a few pairs of socks, and found her hearing aids. She had told me the kerasol cream was on the left side of her bed, on the floor, in a box. I could not find it. I went on the right side of her bed and found some lazy leg cream and brought that. She was happy to get some of her clothes, but I had not gotten the right cream. She knew the cream I had gotten in error was located on the right side of her bed. I told her I would look again.

She was excited to see the DVD player, and I brought her the Downtown Abbey DVD Series on her bed. Then her face turned slightly. Dianne said, "You better take those DVDs and the hearing aids back. Someone here will steal the DVD player, DVDs, and the hearing aids."

Chapter 10: DHS Removed Her

The point of this is that she knew exactly where things were and for what she was asking. She also knew her things would be stolen if I left them there. I went to her house the third day, and, lo and behold, there was the kerasol cream that I had somehow missed! It was in a box with some other items, and yes, on the left side of her bed. I was probably overwhelmed by looking for everything and just didn't see it. I don't know. But she knew exactly where it was and how to describe the location for me.

I went to see Dianne every day until her sons arrived from out of state. I would rub her legs and arms and bring her some lotion or some clothes from the house. She had bed sores on her backside and a light case of shingles. Yes, her bear disappeared.

When Mark, Bryan, and Steve arrived, they ordered a dumpster. I already had a lawn care person come out to mow and trim since the house looked abandoned. The sons came in on a Wednesday and began going through the house where they had grown up. I know it was extremely challenging for them. The sons threw out nearly all the contents of the house. I stayed out of the way; I would have saved many items and found places to donate them, but this wasn't my place, so I left.

It is interesting to note; there was not a purse, wallet, nor identification they could find in her belongings. The heavy-duty furniture and a few lawn care items were left for the Salvation Army and the lawn care person to pick up. I called five charitable organizations asking for pick-up, but they didn't have anyone available or no longer did pick-ups. The sons' mission was to empty the house, get it prepared to sell, go to court, get custody of their mom, and get her the heck out of the state.

When I attended court with the sons, the DHS person who had removed Dianne attended with her lawyer. She was scary-looking—she was a large woman with tattoos all over her arms! It was really just a formality of paperwork and legalese, and it was all over within 30 minutes. We walked out, and Mark asked the DHS representative about the house keys. Ms. Smith said she would return the keys and some other items to the house that afternoon. This was very disturbing! A government authority removed a person from her home, took the keys and a few other items. I mentioned earlier, the sons did not find any identification for her. This posed a problem for admitting her to assisted living in Florida later. Who can say whether other people associated with DHS entered the house in the three-week time frame? Now, let's contrast the story of the sons' father's death with their mother's story.

When their father died alone in Nevada two years earlier, the apartment manager called the county coroner's office. The body was removed, two guns and some money were retrieved, placed in a plastic bag. His door lock was changed, and police tape was placed over the door. When the sons arrived, they were presented with these items and given a new key. The point is, in this case, the premises were secured, unlike what happened with their mother.

The last complication of settling their dad's estate was that the dad's apartment manager allowed the sons to leave their dad's car in the parking lot. After two months passed, the management changed, and the car was towed away. When Bryan called the towing company, they informed him that the car was being held "hostage" for towing and impoundment fees of $5,000. It was a $3,000 car! Bryan told the towing company to keep the car and send him a letter of reclamation. The towing company owner discourteously replied that he wasn't going to send him anything. Bryan had to wrap his head around that. Keep in mind, he's living in another state, handling the last bit of his dad's estate from there, and the car was at an impoundment lot. The next day, Bryan called the towing company. He said that it was fine that they retain the car but that he would be contacting the circuit judge because the judge had to account for all property of the deceased. Only then did the towing company comply and send a letter claiming the car and that no further towing and impoundment fees were due.

I am adding a snippet of the sons' dealings with their dad's estate, as it was complicated, and again, being far away, out of state, and with no legal, financial, or medical documents in order. Dealing with a towing company over your deceased dad's vehicle three months later when living out of state just aggravated an already difficult situation.

Mark and Bryan filed a police report regarding some items that were missing from their mother's house. They didn't know if they were missing before DHS gained entry or afterward. A policeman said there had been some complaints about DHS the past year. They did not find any purses or photo identification in the house.

Steve took Dianne to Florida and put her in an assisted care facility, fifteen minutes away from where he lived. Dianne had purchased a long-term care insurance plan while in her sixties and had continued to pay the premiums. She never made use of the policy. As I mentioned earlier, when I asked her about the home health care agencies, she said they were too expensive. Her insurance would have helped in this case. Once Steve got her situated in the new nursing home in a different state, the policy was activated. Had she used the policy earlier, she would have had a variety of quality caregivers or have been able to move to an assisted living facility.

A week later, in Arkansas, I attended a grand opening of a new retirement facility. It was fabulous! It offered cottages with garages, studios, one, and two-bedroom apartments, a movie room for 100 people, social places, an indoor swimming pool, exercise room, and much more! The ADA studio was 500 square feet for $2,700 a month, including meals. After the tour, I walked out of there and just thought to myself, "God Above! If this woman had signed proper documents, sold her house, and sized down to something like this, it would have saved her and her sons so much agony."

As you read the story of this difficult situation, you might ask yourself these questions. Why might the sons be so disconnected from their mother concerning her physical, emotional, and financial needs? Why did it take them so long to drive from states 1,000 miles away to secure a good living arrangement for their mother? On some level, I suppose that everyone might have been a little at fault, but the primary issue is one of dysfunction within a family. Their mother's pattern of hiding her assets, her true situation, feelings, and needs had been going on for years, so you must conclude that the pervasive problem of poor trust and family communication is the real culprit in this situation and many more like it.

Ultimately, like in all these stories, it is up to the parent to make the decisions.

Below is a letter I later received from Dianne's oldest son, Mark:

> "As you are aware, my mother, Dianne, passed away a few weeks back. I attribute her hastened decline and subsequent death to the trauma imposed on her by inept government institutions. My family lost our mother partially due to stresses produced by the Department of Human Services' actions and inactions, an agency within the State of Arkansas. She rapidly declined from the point DHS removed her by force from her home.
>
> Can you imagine the horror of being forcibly removed from your home by DHS and police officers at the age of 93 without someone familiar present to support and explain the situation? As a result of inept and imperious procedures, my family incurred tens of thousands of dollars in losses and expenditures. The most frightening part is how the process unfolded from beginning to end. The entire process was adversarial. The lack of communication, the dictatorial attitudes of DHS officers, and their lack of oversight were emotionally overwhelming. I nearly had a breakdown due to the frustration and outright fear of losing our mother's freedom. I think it is relevant to discuss my family's background in its service to this country. My father served 26 years in the United States Army. He was decorated 17 times and retired as an Infantry Lt Colonel. He served in combat during WWII, the Korean conflict and completed two Vietnam tours.

Chapter 10: DHS Removed Her

In turn, I picked up where Father left off and served twelve years of active duty, participating in the Cold War and Desert Storm as an Infantry Major. My mother, brothers, and I made sacrifices that only American military families serving during conflicts and wars understand. I am bringing our background into this narrative for this reason. My family sacrificed as many others have, serving this country and living a sacrificial life that included burying our Brothers In Arms. We served with the explicit purpose of preventing the very things we endured during these horrible experiences.

My observation is that the state system of dealing with inferred family problems is not only broken but out of control. In my experience, the Department of Human Services is a bureaucracy that actually does more harm than good. A great quote from the caseworker that sums up the arrogance is, "We have the authority to do what we want." We spent days calling anyone and everyone with nothing but *an incredible runaround*, even at the highest state level. We finally got in the *back door* and spoke to a supervisor. He initially seemed responsive but soon would not return our phone calls.

Even our attorney had severe difficulties communicating with his counterpart DHS attorney. No one would respond and, when they did, they requested us to produce information and action with little preparation at the last minute. My brothers and I all live several states away and could not reasonably deal with their mandated timeline. A very sobering point became increasingly clear. If a family of relatively well-educated and successful professionals with the means to fight has this degree of difficulty, what chance does a citizen of Arkansas without financial means and education have? I am sure many just throw up their hands, fall into depression and give up. I can assure you that I have never experienced anything as mismanaged and overbearing as the Arkansas Department of Human Services in all my military career and my corporate experiences. Below is a snapshot of some of the issues. Otherwise, in detail, these words would become volumes. The caseworker I dealt with was brash, egotistical, arrogant, and showed no sign of empathy. She had an obvious power issue and was seemingly operated with impunity. Her correspondence with us before taking our mother by force was only via text. Communication was, at best cold and after the fact.

Reasonable and empathetic communication would have prevented all stressful outcomes. It all happened so fast, giving us almost no time to react. My mother was in communication with caregiving providers. We even found return messages left on her answering machine from agencies she had contacted.

My mother had a premium long-term care policy that would have taken care of the situation if someone had even bothered to communicate with my brothers or me. It was an absolute insult to my family when we first saw our mother, the wife of a Lt. Colonel, who at one time was presented to the Emperor of Japan during his birthday celebration. We now find her a resident of a nursing home for the indigent. This was a result of the inept egregious actions of the Department of Human Services. I think I'd rather call it the Department of Inhumane Services. After way too much time and expense, we finally got control of the situation. We placed Mother in a superior senior care facility in Jacksonville, FL, activating her excellent long-term care insurance policy to mitigate the expense.

Chapter 10: DHS Removed Her

The State of Arkansas Department of Human Services spent thousands of taxpayer dollars exacerbating a problem that really didn't exist and could have been easily resolved. If only reasonable and good judgment had been their focus! If any proprietary protocols and fact-finding had been part of the scenario. If they even attempted reasonable and proper communication with the family.

In addition to all of the stressful happenings, I observed a total lack of security procedures regarding the safety of her belongings. I was surprised when the caseworker asked questions about my mother's finances. She expressed that she had gone through papers to find financial documents regarding my mother's income. This was just after they removed my mother, and she took her to a mental facility for *observation*. What right did she have going through personal documents at mother's house, and who witnessed this process? Note: throughout my dealings, I found no indication of supervision, oversight, checks, and balances were ensuring the accountability of the DHS officials.

Another disturbing observation was after the court proceedings ended, the caseworker said she had some of my mother's belongings and that she would bring them to her house. She brought them by and handed me a plain envelope with no seals, no signatures, and didn't have me sign for it. Once again, there was clearly no accountability. The security of the house was compromised for the entire time we were fighting for the custody of our mother. I inquired about the security of the house, and the caseworker replied, "I got the keys from the caregiver." I assumed the locks had been changed, and they had initiated proper protocols to safeguard the contents. I later found out that the caseworker asked the neighbors to monitor the house. I assume they had a key but were completely unsupervised. The caseworker had access and had gone through documents. Was someone with her while she snooped through Mom's life? Was there any oversight of her actions? Reasonable communication could have been prevented this.

In my professional background, being a financial advisor and consultant, I would never be alone dealing with someone's personal documents without a witness. I certainly would not take custody of anything without following a chain of proper protocols. In no professional capacity have I been exposed to such a lack of accountability. Upon our arrival at Mom's house, we found a large number of items missing. I did an inventory based upon receipts and memory and determined a low estimate of some $60,000 in jewelry, coins, bullion, and collectibles missing amid a whole room of empty boxes. A file cabinet safe even disappeared. We don't know if DHS had anything to do with the missing items or if they had disappeared with an unscrupulous caregiver. I made a police report. We had found empty boxes where items had been purchased. One, even more telling, was a box for a car battery charger. My mother hadn't driven in years!

Also, as a result of this crisis, we had to rush the sale of the house under duress, which created an additional loss of thousands of dollars. Thankfully, we had a caring and responsible realtor, the author of this book, who worked very hard to dispose of unwanted items, get the property in presentable condition, and ready to sell. Legal fees devoured even more funds.

I just lost my mother and am still recovering, even more from what I went through due to the imperious Gestapo-like

Chapter 10: DHS Removed Her

conduct of the Arkansas Department of Human Services. I just hope that this will find someone with enough compassion and will to get this out-of-control agency under control. My take is that the entire culture of this organization is broken. We can make excuses regarding their funding, but this agency's actions and attitude are a slap in the face to the basic civil liberties my family spent their lives serving to uphold.

Sincerely

Mark G."

Chapter 11

Relative Rip-off

My story was born in the deep south of America, in the midst of live oak trees and swamps. As I grew up with two brothers and two sisters, the word swamp, became more meaningful. My parents were middle-class people, Father having had a good job that included a retirement pension. I suppose my childhood was nothing unusual, but growing up in the deep south gave me a good look at both rich and poor and the advantages and disadvantages of each.

The medical world caught my spirit, so after high school and college, I went to my chosen professional school. I married my first wife while in school, and she helped support my education. Only my youngest brother and I pursued a good career, with the rest subsisting on society's hand-outs and my parent's generosity. The only time I ever asked my parents for more than the usual household sustenance was while in school. When I entered professional school, I asked Father for $50 a month to help with expenses. He reluctantly agreed to that but was not very nice about it. After I finished school, I began paying him back.

The years passed, and so did my father. My career was becoming established and going well, so I began sending Mother $400 each month to help with expenses, attempting to elevate her lifestyle. There were times that I sent her twice that amount. Then, the swamp began to grow. My youngest sister, who lived only a stone's throw away, began coming into

Mother's house and asking her for money, usually saying that the police were going to arrest her for writing hot checks if she didn't cough up some cash. A few hits upon Mother for $1500 soon ballooned into amounts that she could never pay back. One time, when I went to visit Mom, she pulled me aside and told me, "Your sister owes me $20,000, and I want you to meet with her." She didn't show up for the meeting.

I understand parents' general desire to help their needy children, but Mother didn't learn anything from the continual coercion by her offspring. Once, while flying home after a visit, I thought, you know, it's time to take control of her money. Well, as many of you can probably relate, that is usually a very difficult task.

I called Mother and told her that I would be happy to help her manage her money and put a stop to her children's taking advantage of her, but to do that, I must have control of her checking account. She said she'd think about it. The next day she called and said, "I've been thinking about this, and I refuse to do that." I continued sending Mom $400 every month, which by then was up to over $50,000. Eventually, she moved in with my younger sister in Florida. I helped my Florida sister a few times. I lent her $5,000 one time.

Mother decided that she wanted to sell her house while I was looking at a deal with a doctor in my hometown. I had a verbal agreement with her that she would repay part of the money I had been giving her through the years when she sold the house. We agreed upon $40,000. I looked at her bank account, and more than $70,000 was there. Suddenly, it disappeared. My younger sister, in Florida, had become a derelict by then, and I am quite sure she somehow got her hands on that money. I was never given a satisfactory answer to what happened, but no one will ever convince me otherwise. She passed away some years later, and I never saw a penny of that money.

Keep in mind, the swamp contained three siblings. My youngest brother and I were the only self-sufficient offspring. My younger brother had his own special way of taking advantage of Mom. He was mostly

Chapter 11: Relative Rip-Off

what many would describe as a bum, so he was frequently looking for a free meal. He made a habit of stopping by two or three times a week and pretend to want to have lunch with her. He would get lunch, bring it to her, and they would eat. Then, he would get money from her, who knows how much. I remember that he was once offered a regular job building wrought iron fences. He wouldn't commit to regular responsibility because he didn't want to work more than 8 hours a month, let alone 8 hours a day! After Mother finally went to a nursing facility, diagnosed with Alzheimer's disease, he never visited her again. Father's retirement benefits funded Mom's nursing home care.

When Mother first entered the nursing home, her checks were still coming to her address. My sister took the first three checks and cashed them. This led to the nursing facility limiting Mother's access to all their best services. In the end, they garnished all of Mother's income from Father's retirement benefits, so we siblings never saw any of that money ever again. Only then did the fraud stop.

While many of my family memories are tainted with fraud and abuse, I do have one memory that I dearly cherish. My youngest brother, the other responsible one, and I had a satisfying ongoing relationship. I made a habit every night of pouring myself a glass of scotch whiskey, settling into a comfortable recliner, and calling him at 9:20 p.m. when he went on shift working at his post-retirement job at a state turnpike authority. We had many wonderful conversations as he monitored cars going through the pay stations.

Why do you think Mother allowed her children and grandchildren to take advantage of her? My sister's daughter came to her house one day and asked to see her diamond wedding ring. Mom gave it to her to look at, and she rushed it to a waiting boyfriend. They pawned it. What kind of pain does it take to wake up the elderly? What kind of fraud must happen before enough is enough? One's need to be in control and vital in the eyes of their family or the caregivers frequently makes logic a fleeting cloud of smoke.

You might wonder if life has been good. Well, yes, it has. I've had many wonderful experiences both professionally and personally. I am now married to a wonderful woman, and life is, once again, on track. The takeaway from all the above is just this: **Take Nothing for Granted and Get Your Affairs in Order!**

Of course, I must say, life is not perfect and never will be. In the Bible, David prayed to his God, "Lord, do not set my feet in a place too great for me." Well, God has set my feet in many good places. It is just that life occasionally got in the way, and my reality came face to face with its problems. I am thankful to have survived the trauma and have moved forward to a more peaceful and fulfilling life.

Chapter 12

Crisis Related Events Lead to Losses

Post World War II was a time of new beginnings. The freshness and space of the suburbs were becoming appealing to young families. The thought of having a rather sleek family car and a pleasant place to live while working and raising a family was high on the American priority list. Consumerism became a better-known word, and the products and delights that American ingenuity brought to the marketplace fueled the purchasing products fire.

This was a time I like to call the pre-technology era where retail managers usually did all the daily tasks of running a business with a pencil, paper, adding machines, a smile, and hard work. It was a day when marketing was done by hand, not by design software on a computer. Store managers cut and pasted pictures together to make newspaper ads. They hand-painted signs with reusable and refillable magic marker-like pens on yellow poster board paper. Running a business was an open-ended job where you could enjoy working all you could stand. There were never enough hours in the day to get it all done. Customers loved shopping in stores with a bounty of ready-made products and became accustomed to the personalities and skills of these talented retailers.

During those days, men were usually the boss of things, the head of the household, and the primary decision-maker. Many men didn't even involve their wives and families in the process. These supportive women frequently worked doing secretarial chores in the business, usually without pay, just to help their husbands and spend a little time with them. The children in the family often helped as well, sweeping floors and washing windows, receiving a piece of candy or a small allowance as their reward. In short, retail managers and their families lived lives built around their businesses, frequently with only a little time left over to be a deacon in the local Baptist church.

The particular man in this story was a driven, hardworking fellow who worked for a five-and-dime chain in the 1950s. He developed his interest in retail from an uncle who owned a family clothing store. Later on, his work in the drug store and the five-and-dime businesses paved the way for him to become a manager for one of the more successful 20th-century American chains. Yes, an American dream came true. Back then, true grit and an extreme sense of urgency when running a business were highly valued traits. He had those qualities, and they caught the eye of his future boss.

You can probably imagine that this family moved around a lot before landing the job he had always wanted. While he began working at a very low salary, he believed in his company, eventually buying into the business. He even borrowed money to add to his ownership percentage. His talents and work ethic led him to become a district manager, having several stores under his command. His family time was extremely limited, and like many of the era, he did not involve or educate his family in the ways of the world and money. They were sheltered and well cared for, so they followed the leadership guidance and didn't question the path, a familiar scenario in the days before feminine independence.

As stated earlier, he was a driven man, and like most of us, his upbringing had plenty of bumps in its road. He overcame all those hurdles that served as confirmation of what he didn't want and worked very diligently toward what he did want. Over time he amassed a very large fortune.

Then, boom, without warning, he, unfortunately, suffered a massive heart attack. He was kept alive for a while but then taken off life support.

Chapter 12: Crisis Related Event Leads to Losses

The shock of this had widespread ramifications besides the personal grief. This dedicated family man took excellent care of his wife and daughters but never educated them about investments and financial discernment.

They were left with massive amounts of money but no financial prowess. They were also extremely private about their wealth and wary of allowing anyone to know of their resources. All in all, the family of the deceased were prime targets for unscrupulous husbands and con artist money managers.

After their strong provider's untimely death, the survivors were suddenly thrust into the world of wealth management. None of them had a realistic idea of where to begin. Illnesses struck the family, causing the death of one daughter, Ann, and further distraction from financial management.

The other daughter, Suzanna, married a man who, unbeknownst to her, was a drug user and wife beater. During an explosive episode, he broke her jaw in so many places that it took years and several surgeries to repair the damage. Divorce ended that relationship.

Suzanna and her mother, Maureen, lived near one another but had no idea how to manage their wealth. They had often heard their deceased leader speak of diversifying his investment portfolio but didn't have the understanding of risks involved and the occasionally unscrupulous money managers that might cross their path. The family had been doing business with a local insurance agent in their town who seemed reliable. Suzanna went to the office to do some business, but her agent was in a meeting. When the meeting was finished, a financial seminar, the agent came out with the money manager in charge of the meeting. Susanna had told her agent that her mother was looking for a financial advisor. He used the opportunity to introduce Suzanna to the assumed expert. As they got to know each other, she invited her mother to meet him later. He was very personable, and they both really liked him. Their relationship continued, and trust in him grew, a trust that allowed one of the most unscrupulous con artists imaginable to walk into their lives. A really fine con artist can smell money and naiveté.

The money manager inserted himself into his unsuspecting clients' lives. He helped them with personal matters, helped Suzanna with the divorce and separation from her abusive husband. In short, he quickly became a trusted friend, to the point that he was looked upon as "family." As fate would have it, Maureen was diagnosed with ovarian cancer and given six months to live during the spawning of this relationship. There were documents signed in a hospital bed. The emotions of dying were mixed with how to invest for the future.

The frantic nature of this scenario aided the aggressive con artist in luring his prey. He rather quickly became in charge of millions of dollars. These were all crisis-related events that moved the family into the clutches of an egregious criminal.

In a twist of fate, Maureen did not die but beat ovarian cancer. She not only survived that cancer but, a few years later, colon cancer as well. She lived another ten years before leukemia finally decided her fate. The money manager had always made a habit of depositing whatever money the ladies needed into their accounts when requested. However, account statements were never provided despite requests for them. The attitude that their almost family member and trusted friend would never do anything to hurt them prevailed.

He flew them around in an airplane (purchased with their money!), he established a foundation at a local hospital in the family name. He appeared to be "on top of things and in control."

Then, one morning, the FBI knocked on the door of Suzanna's house. They informed her that they were investigating the money manager. Unfortunately, the money manager had another client. They subsequently went to the other client's home, telling her this gut-wrenching news. Initially, Suzanna and Maurene didn't believe the suspicions of the FBI were true, but, as time went on, the truth became known. She and her mother were devastated and nearly destitute.

The synopsis of what happened to this con artist is as follows. It turned out that he had fooled everyone. He had only a high school education and absolutely no experience in the investment world. He obtained a partner who provided the necessary licenses. Like many, after being caught by the FBI, his explanation was "bad investment." He was charged with various counts of loan and investment fraud, with money laundering and mail fraud being among the charges. He was originally sentenced to 144 months in prison but, after agreeing to testify against his partner, this was lowered to around 60 months. He was ordered to repay his former clients millions of dollars. However, none of his clients have seen a significant amount of that judgment. Some money was recouped by suing other involved entities and selling property, but only a very small percentage of the total loss has been recovered.

Today, he is a free man. Is he looking for new cons? Many of these unscrupulous predators are lurking in the shadows. The destruction of a lifetime of amassing wealth can happen to anyone. Avoiding insidious situations like the events described above must be a priority for all family retirement and estate planning. *DO NOT* wait for a crisis-related event.

Chapter 13

The Doctor Intercedes

My dad, Charlie, was close to the age of many victims in this book. They were born in the Depression Era. They worked hard, most were loyal to their family, made deals with a handshake, and trusted others.

Dad told me he started his business by borrowing $500 from his mother-in-law. He started what became a thriving multimillion-dollar business in Dallas. My parents lived in an influential neighborhood and were economically and socially successful for many years. My siblings and I followed in their footsteps into the world of real estate, construction, and accounting.

In 2020, Mom was diagnosed with dementia. Dad did everything he could for her. After a while, it just became too much for him to handle. We eventually agreed to send her to a care facility that could better care for her. Turmoil and confusion ensued, and after a few weeks, we brought her back home.

Dad then hired an in-home care agency. They provided three women to care for them. Initially, it seemed things were going well, and their needs were being met. Like other home care agencies, they would cook meals, keep Mom company, help her bathe, make doctor appointments and oversee medications.

About four months into their employment things began spiraling out of control. One of the workers, Jody, persuaded Dad to hire her directly, bypassing the Agency. Dad paid a fee to the Agency and agreed to retain the other two workers as Agency employees.

She took complete control of my parents. She became the household manager, so to speak. She began brainwashing Dad, getting control of his mind. She convinced him to give her credit cards, access to their computer, insurance information, and the list goes on. Unbeknownst to us, Jody began criticizing and belittling me, my brother, and my sister. She convinced Dad we were only after his money. Probably, like some of the other stories, it must have been a daily conversation.

We believe Jody transmitted Covid 19 to our parents. She had not been on schedule the week earlier, and then returned. They became so ill that Jody finally summoned an ambulance to rush them to the nearest hospital. Jody tried to control everything the nurses did. She said they weren't correctly caring for them. She claimed that she knew better than them. Jody defied the doctor's orders and got Dad released too soon and took him home where his care was completely insufficient, slowing his recovery. In fact, Dad fired his PCP, Dr. Cheryl, because of the conflicts between her and Jody! Dr. Cheryl had been Dad's PCP for twenty years. Dr. Cheryl told my sister, who had Dad's POA that she thought about reporting Jody but didn't feel she had enough evidence at that point.

After Dad was back home, on one occasion, Jody left him in an upstairs room with the door locked. He began having difficulty breathing so much that he couldn't get to his phone or the door. We don't know how long he suffered, but another caregiver happened by and heard Dad's labored breathing and cries for help. She didn't have keys for the interior locks that Jody had gotten installed. She called Jody, who came over, and unlocked the door. She had had all the locks in the house changed, and only she had the keys.

We went from a very loving and welcoming family to a nightmare. Dad even put signs in the windows telling his family not to enter his house. We had not seen our parents for months due to Covid 19 and him not wanting anything to do with us!

Chapter 13: The Doctor Intercedes

She even persuaded Dad to remove my sister as Dad's POA. He opted for his brother, Jerry, to become his POA. That was done in December 2020 with a different attorney than he normally used. We were not aware of this until later.

Dad and his brother, Jerry, grew up together, playing football and always talked about the pro leagues. Every Super Bowl, there was an ongoing conversation about who might win and why. Well, this past Super Bowl, Dad wouldn't even answer Jerry's calls. He had shut him out as well.

What eventually and finally turned this horrible situation around was Dad's heart doctor, Dr. Samantha. She emphatically told Dad that Jody was killing him! Jody was not giving him the proper medical attention or medications. Once Dad realized what was happening, he fired Jody because both doctors had told him the same thing.

It was good to get our dad back! But it was really too late. He had degenerated so badly and, subsequently, was hospitalized. After readmission to the hospital for a few weeks, he was then transferred to an acute rehab hospital for forty-five days to receive palliative care.

The past four months of shuffling between hospitals and rehabs had been too much. We, as a family, had not been in a position to do anything due to Jody's brainwashing and the isolation due to the Covid 19 requirements. We also couldn't talk to him because of all the drugs they pumped into him.

Dad experienced hallucinations from long-term IV Morphine use and possibly a syndrome related to being in a hospital for so long. When the hospital staff began detoxing him, his hallucinations worsened. He began tearing off his oxygen and whatever else he could get ahold of. He had to be restrained, and frankly, they were fairly rough with him. He was not doing well at all. He called and asked for his pastor to come. He called me the day his pastor came and wanted me to come over to spend the night with him. I was very surprised, but he wanted family support once again.

He wanted to speak to me in private because he wanted to tell me the vivid details of his Morphine induced hallucinations. He proceeded to tell me that he had been kidnapped. They had broken out all his teeth and cut out his tongue. I stopped him, looked at him straight in the eyes, and told him he was safe. I explained to him that he was hallucinating. They're bringing you off the medication, and nobody has harmed you. This has happened to you in the hospital. I got a piece of paper and wrote, "You have not been kidnapped. You are safe. Your family loves you."

His face began to turn bright. He said, "Oh, Kate! I can't believe you're telling me this. Please take me home. You've given me a reason to live now!" As soon as I convinced him that he was safe and none of the things he described were true or happening, he began to cry. He said that he now wanted to live. It was like a God was there miracle!

After our miracle, the next day, the doctors were astonished. He went from ready to die to ready to live. He wanted to get stronger and go home. He wanted a new truck and a new horse. Everyone was amazed!

One helpful thing I noticed was that most of Dad's hallucinations were related to situations or things that either had happened to him while he was in a hospital or being moved between hospitals over the past few months. I wonder how many people are shuffled through the system like a chess game? I explained those situations to him, helping him see that what I was saying was true. His desire to die had been because he truly believed his hallucinations and bad dreams were reality. For some reason, although others heard the same words, no one took his pleas for help and comments about what he thought was happening to him seriously. After my visit that evening, my dad had a new lease on life and fought even harder to get better.

He told me he wanted me to write about his experience to inspire people and also warn them. Their loved ones might be wanting to die because they are hallucinating. This could be the only reason they want to die.

Chapter 13: The Doctor Intercedes

Dad had a couple of restful days before he passed. Mom is still in her home with a different care agency. We haven't told her that Dad has passed. No telling what would happen if she realized that, when she has dementia.

Since Dad's passing, we have learned that Jody had purchased a $10,000 security system for the house that we were able to return. She had taken out many loans online using his credit cards and social security number. She had complete control of our parents' lives and healthcare and isolated them from us completely.

I filed a detailed complaint against Jody with the Texas Nurses Aid Registry. They published a phone number for complaints as well as provide an address for written complaints. They said they would set up a visit with an investigator. We'll see if I get a response.

Meanwhile, Jody is still out there, probably caring for someone else now.

Chapter 14

They're Only as Good as the Company They Work For

I have been a Certified Nursing Assistant for just over a year in the State of Florida. I began this career late in life, but I certainly have found that I enjoy helping people and doing the best I can for these "old souls". They've paid their dues throughout their life and at this time, they are likely to be so undeservingly lonely and vulnerable.

In my short tenure, I've noticed many atrocities or violations that shouldn't be a part of caregiving. I mean, that is the point, isn't it? Do you care?? Or, is it about the money??

Below are some examples.

If you see a trash bag being brought in, perhaps it's the caregiver's laundry she'll do while the client is watching tv or asleep. Yes, she'll bring her dirty clothes, use your laundry soap, machine and water. Do you mind? Maybe not. But, were you asked?

Some of the caregivers work at other jobs, where they can get benefits, so they tend to sleep on this job! Being a caregiver means you are an independent contractor with no employer provided benefits.

The agency administrators usually call the client, in advance, to make an appointment to see the client and ask how the client is doing with the caregivers. Why is there an advance appointment needed? If you really want to see what's going on with your employees, shouldn't you just show up, unannounced??

The Admin wouldn't care to look around to see if the house is clean, the bed is made. "Nope, I don't need to see it" was the response.

"Do you want to look at the daily care sheets?"

"No, not really." The Admin replied.

I've known caregivers that show up all the time in their flip flops, stretch pants and t-shirt. Sometimes they show up with wet hair! Once they know an Admin is arriving, they'll bring their uniform in from the car, with their name badge, put on makeup and do their hair.

The Admin would not ask the caregiver to leave the room so the Admin could have a one on one conversation with the client. Do you think the client would say anything negative with the caregiver In the room? They need to give the client an opportunity to talk with the Admin privately! Does this sound like the Admin cares?

Speaking of daily care sheets, they are the most critical part of communication between caregivers regarding the daily care of the client. I once wasn't available for my client for four days. When I returned and reviewed the care sheets, the only thing I read was "All good!" I found a new medication for my client on the table. I texted one of the caregivers, to which she replied, "Oh yeah, she's got a kidney infection." Gee, do you think that might have needed to be noted on those intendedly useful care sheets? Such a disconnect in communication within this industry!

I think it would be a great idea if caregivers could fill out the daily care sheets online where concerned family members and agencies could immediately access them at the end of the day. With this tool they would know who was with the loved one at any certain time, what the client ate, how they felt, if they had bowel movement that day, etc. A family member had said, my mom didn't eat Tuesday evening. Well, how might one know who was on duty that particular evening?

The agency just sends a weekly bill to the family member without detailed information about their loved one.

It is the agencies' job to check in on their employees and clients.

I met a caregiver who was taking care of a friend of mine. This woman was very nice to me, offered me something to eat and drink. Honestly,

Chapter 14: They're Only as Good as the Company They Work For

a "red flag" went up with me. Why would this person want to be so kind to me? Watching her is what motivated me to consider this profession. I knew I could do a better job than what I was witnessing.

For example, the caregiver would go to the grocery store and, of course, use my friend's credit card to get her groceries. But then, she would go back in and shop for herself, with my friend's credit card! She'd put them in her car and take them home. After taking care of herself, all on company time, she would deliver my friend's groceries to her! My friend always wondered why this task took her so long when she could almost see the grocery store from where she lives!

When my sweet lady client, Teresa, who is 88 and uses a walker, needed to take a shower in the evening, I would ask if she wanted me to wait for her in the bathroom.

She replied, "Yes, that would be great, in case I fall."

"Aren't the other caregivers in the bathroom with you?"

Teresa has to step over the shower stop ledge and get her walker.

"So you step over the ledge in the shower and get your walker and your "helper" doesn't offer you a hand or help dry you off?"

"No, they sit in the adjacent room watching tv or messing with their phone."

There are so many who take advantage of this unmonitored situation. These needy clients could not be more vulnerable!

Teresa has mild dementia. Sometimes she misses something or maybe it has been misplaced. Or maybe, it's just gone. I went to the bank with her at Christmas time last year to get $500. I asked her why she wanted to do that and she replied, "Because it's Christmas! I just like to have it because I like to send it to the grandkids."

"Well, it's my money."

Ok, we went to the bank and withdrew the $500 and then, returned to her home.

I sent her son a message, "Your mom withdrew $500 for your kids' Christmas."

He responded that his mom hasn't sent his kids $500 for the last 15 years!

I then told Teresa, "Good news! We can take the $500 back to the bank."

She responded, "Oh, OK!!!" She didn't remember withdrawing the money earlier.

She had a small ceramic dish near her bed with her wedding rings and a cross in it. "Teresa, why are your rings here?"

"I don't know what to do with them," she replied.

"Well, let's just tuck these away in a drawer."

Then, I sent her daughter a note telling her where they were located. There is a lot of "caring" to be done in this caregiver job. You just have to care enough to do it.

When the agency was trying to find some caregivers for Teresa, four women showed up for her to meet. Only one woman shook her hand and introduced herself. The other three did not.

The "personable" caregiver told Teresa, "I just want to make sure you're going to be comfortable and happy. What do you like?"

"I like to have dinner at 6 p.m." That's the one that I want. Teresa told me later. She "won her over" with her personality.

However, that caregiver took care of Teresa for only a week. The following week, the agency gave her someone else who didn't mind staying until 8 p.m. at night. If you had a good client like Teresa, wouldn't you want to work something out? Teresa was so upset.

"Did I say something wrong?"

"No, Teresa, she just wanted to be closer to home. Her car headlight wasn't working and she didn't feel comfortable driving at night." I replied.

"Well, I would've fixed her headlight!"

The agency took it upon themselves to move the personable caregiver on to someone else and, later, she moved on to a different agency. She could have been with Teresa and could have had a good stable income while caring for her. A win-win situation.

Chapter 14: They're Only as Good as the Company They Work For

The rewarding part of all of this, is that I can be there for someone in need. It is worth all the money in the world. To think a "caregiver" can take advantage of such vulnerable people, they're just going to hell. If you have your head on straight, you actually care, then they're ok. It's one of the nicest things one can do for another. There's nothing more rewarding than this.

– Debby B., Florida licensed CNA

Chapter 15

My Parents Did It Right

My father came to me when he was 80 years old and said: "I will no longer help you in the family business, and your mother and I are moving to a retirement home." I must admit that I was more than a little taken aback that day, but, in retrospect, those words were the beginning of a string of excellent decisions that my father made in his last 15 years.

He was tired and no longer wanted any responsibility in the business he had started some 60 years earlier. He grew weary of taking care of the home and yard where they lived for about 45 years. He and my mother had traveled to most of the places they had wanted to go, so I guess it was time to narrow their world and live in a community of fairly successfully retired folks over the age of 65.

This began a fifteen-year journey toward the end of life for them, but it was an interesting and excellent way to spend those last years. They made good friends, hung out with a regular group at mealtime, and even got involved with some of the volunteer activities around the facility. This beautiful retirement village included a very nice apartment or a duplex if you so desired, many organized activities, transportation to various events, doctor's appointments, shopping, etc., a dementia center, and a skilled care nursing home. They both took advantage of all of these amenities, with the exception of the dementia center.

Good decision #1:

They chose a beautiful and efficient place where they could spend their last years. It saved my brother and me mountains of work in taking care of many of their needs.

Good decision #2:

One Thanksgiving Day after my mother had passed, at 87, my brother invited Dad to join them for the annual feast. It was an unusually cold Thanksgiving, so Dad bundled up and drove to their house. He was around 90. When he got out of his car in the driveway, he fell and, being somewhat feeble by then, could not get up. He had left his cell phone in the car, so he could not call for help. He laid there in the cold for almost 30 minutes before my brother became concerned and went looking for him. A few days later, I walked into his apartment, and he handed me the car keys. He asked me to take him where he needed to go from that point forward, and I gladly took on the assignment.

Good decision #3:

When he was in his late 80's, he asked me if I would take over his financial investments and all financial activities. I did so, and he gave both my brother and me equal POA over all his affairs. Since he had two responsible offspring who got along well, he avoided putting his assets in a trust and simply made all his accounts POD, Payable on Death, equally to each of his sons. After he passed, it probably took my brother and me around a half-day to settle 95% of his estate.

Good decision #4:

As I previously mentioned, the facility he and Mother moved into was very nice, so friends and relatives naturally assumed that they were in very good shape, financially speaking. That being true, frequently, they were asked by needy friends and relatives to loan them money. Dad turned them all down without his sons having to get involved.

Chapter 15: My Parents Did It Right

Good decision #5:

As time marched relentlessly on, Dad became weaker and, as one might guess, fell in his apartment early one morning. He pushed his emergency button that all residents wore, and the facility nurse responded quickly. At that time, they decided that he was only bruised and thought he might be alright. As the day progressed, his pain worsened, so he called me and told me the situation. I alerted the medical staff at the facility once again, and they ordered an ambulance. At the hospital, they decided that he had fractured his hip. Surgery was scheduled the next day, and he survived that, but he experienced shortness of breath during the recovery phase. The hospital staff missed those symptoms at first, so I summoned them, and they got to work on him. He had had a slight heart attack. However, after becoming stable, he seemed to begin improving. After a few days, he was moved back to his retirement facility, but not to his apartment. He was placed in their skilled care section, where he could stay for 90 days in accordance with Medicare rules while deciding if he could go back to independent living. After much wavering and consternation, he decided to give up his apartment and live in the nursing home. He remained there in a semi-private room the last three years of his life, passing at 95.

Dad made these major decisions during his last 15 years, but I'm sure there were many more small ones that complimented these large choices. Dad realized and respected the lives of those charged with caring for him, and he did not want to burden them. All of his actions were made with those issues in mind. I was amazingly fortunate to have had a father like him. He made his final days as pleasant as possible, and I cherish the many conversations we had during those days. I hope I was helpful to him, but one thing is certain. He was a blessing to me.

Max Ryan, the author's husband.

Chapter 16

NewsFlashes

Woman indicted on multiple counts of elder abuse

A Baldwin County grand jury has indicted a 62-year-old Milledgeville woman on multiple counts of elder abuse. An in-home security surveillance camera reportedly captured the incidents as they unfolded, local authorities say. Grand jurors returned a nine-count indictment against Cora Mildred Mason, of the 100 block of Merry Drive, during court proceedings in Baldwin County Superior Court on Tuesday, according to records filed in the office of Baldwin County Superior Court Clerk Mitch Longino.

She was charged with nine counts of exploitation and intimidation of a disabled adult, elder person, or resident. According to an initial incident report filed by Baldwin County Sheriff's Office Deputy Jeffrie Veal, the charges against the defendant, a former employee with Primecare Home Care Services, stem from incidents involving an 87-year-old local woman. Mason was taken into custody a short time after the deputy learned what had taken place. She was jailed in the Baldwin County Law Enforcement Center.

Veal said in her report that after she received a call to go to a residence off Vinson Highway that she talked with the victim's daughter, as well as the manager of the health care service. During a conversation with the victim's daughter, Veal said the woman told her that she discovered her mother on the floor when she arrived home. The caregiver reportedly said the elderly victim had slid off the sofa as she attempted to get up to go to the restroom. The woman told the deputy that her mother refused to allow the caregiver to help her off the floor. Veal said in her report that the woman thought that was odd, so she and her husband decided to review the in-home security surveillance footage.

According to the incident report, the video captured water being thrown into the face of the victim and Mason reportedly yelling and shaking a finger in the face of the woman she was supposed to be caring for. "You can clearly see the victim retreating as much as possible on the sofa," Veal said in her report. "Then, Mason pushes a card table away from in front of (the victim) and slaps her several times across the face. It appears that Mason continues to yell at (the victim), and then she reaches over and grabs (the victim) by the shoulder and arm, and pulls her in an upward manner." Veal said once Mason managed almost to get the victim into a standing position, she turned her loose. The deputy said she later informed Detective Capt. Brad King about the incidents and assigned Detectives Robert Butch and Reid White to investigate the case further.

*

Death of disabled Boise man put in scalding bath was 'horrific accident,' defense says
RUTH BROWN Idaho Statesman Nov 8, 2019

BOISE— The former home health aide accused of putting a disabled Boise man in an extremely hot bath—resulting in his death—is back in Ada County after being arrested in California.

Authorities booked Omar Hamadi, 24, into Ada County Jail on the afternoon of Nov 8 after he was charged with neglect or abuse of a

Chapter 16: Newsflashes

vulnerable adult. He appeared in court Friday and had his bond set at $10,000.

Hamadi is accused of putting Benjamin Reed, 38, into a bathtub of "scalding hot water" on May 16, under the circumstances likely to produce "great bodily harm or death," according to a copy of his criminal complaint. Hamadi reportedly worked as a home health aide for A Caring Hand in Boise, a home health care agency.

The Boise Police Department confirmed that Reed was hospitalized on May 16 after being put in hot water and was transported to a burn unit at a hospital in Salt Lake City, where he died on May 27.

Reed's roommate previously told the Idaho Statesman that Reed couldn't walk or take care of himself due to Huntington's disease. Huntington's is a fatal, incurable genetic disorder that breaks down nerve cells in the brain, according to the Huntington's Disease Society of America. It erodes a person's physical and mental abilities. Symptoms usually appear between the ages of 30 and 50 and worsen over a 10-to-25-year period.

A warrant was issued for Hamadi's arrest on Aug 30, but he wasn't apprehended until October when law enforcement located him in San Diego. Police said that Hamadi had moved to California and that they needed to arrange for extradition back to Idaho.

Hamadi's supporters have retained defense attorney Jon Cox. Cox said in court Friday that Hamadi has cooperated with law enforcement since learning that there was a warrant for his arrest. Hamadi called the Ada County Sheriff's Office himself when he learned of the warrant, Cox said.

Cox said that Hamadi is not guilty of a crime and that Reed's death "at the most is a horrific accident."

Abuse of a vulnerable adult is punishable by up to 10 years in prison.

~ * ~

Attacking the Problem of Elder Abuse in Shelby County | Opinion
Let's all work in any way we can to prevent elder abuse before it happens.

Amy Weirich, Guest Columnist

(Amy Weirich is District Attorney General for Tennessee's 30th Judicial District, Shelby County.)

Earlier this year, a caregiver for an 87-year-old South Memphis woman with dementia pled guilty to stealing $12,600 from her and forging papers to change the title on her car. The woman was moved from her home to a Christian care facility after she was found highly intoxicated and covered in filth.

In another case, a man pled guilty in April to beating and raping a 73-year-old woman in her assisted-living apartment in the Medical Center area. The man knocked on her door, forced his way inside, and struck her in the head repeatedly. He took a short nap before leaving.

And last year, a long-time caregiver for an elderly neighbor admitted beating, kicking, and even using a bullwhip on the 71-year-old man if he did not take his medicine or for no reason at all. The victim's home in the University of Memphis area was in deplorable condition and the victim, who suffered numerous broken bones and bruises, died shortly after being hospitalized. The caregiver pled guilty to voluntary manslaughter, aggravated assault, vulnerable-adult neglect, abuse, and exploitation.

We've been too accustomed to these crimes.

These are just a few of the criminal cases we see far too often in the courts of Shelby County each year. Perhaps even more alarming is that statistics on elder abuse suggest that only one out of 14 cases are ever reported. (The abuse involving the bullwhip continued for 11 years before the battered victim turned up in an emergency room.)

Prosecutors in our Special Victims Unit handle nearly 75 cases each year in which an elderly person is the victim of physical or financial crimes. In some cases, we take a deposition in case an elderly victim becomes unable to testify. The under-reported problem of elder abuse is growing here and across the country as our aging population climbs.

The Tennessee District Attorney General's Conference has worked diligently over the past four years to strengthen, revise and update criminal statutes pertaining to elder abuse. This has resulted in greater protections for the elderly and vulnerable and better tools for prosecutors to hold offenders responsible.

You soon will be seeing public service announcements in our campaign to bring greater awareness to the problem of elder abuse.

How can we give elders a voice?

As many as one of every 10 Americans over the age of 60 have experienced some form of elder abuse. Yet victims often are afraid and unable to report the abuse or will not assist in prosecutions because of their dependence or trust in the abuser. With more than 150,000 local residents in that over-60 population, these disturbing statistics have sparked some important conversations and actions in Memphis and Shelby County.

In 2011, the Plough Foundation experienced an increase in grant requests on aging-related issues. After performing in-depth research on the elder community several years later, Plough began funding CREA (the Coordinated Response to Elder Abuse). Since 2015, more than 25 local government and nonprofit agencies have been collaborating to combat elder abuse and improve these older adults' protection.

One key nonprofit member, Meritan, has served more than 100 clients with homemaker services, nursing and physician in-home visits, and emergency housing when a client's abuse requires immediate intervention and removal.

The local Vulnerable Adult Protective Investigative Team (VAPIT), which includes representatives from my office, CREA, local law enforcement, and Adult Protective Services, regularly meets to discuss abuse, neglect, and exploitation referrals. Again, the generous Plough Foundation leadership has been there with grant support.

The Baptist Elder Abuse Curriculum at Baptist Memorial Healthcare receives national recognition for its program for training healthcare personnel to detect, treat and prevent elder abuse. Ferrell Moore, RN, CRN, and Laura Brown, LCSW, who both developed the curriculum, now serve on the National Collaboratory to Address Elder Mistreatment with national experts in the field of elder abuse.

We also have the Senior Protection Coalition (SPC), which includes elected officials, law enforcement, healthcare executives, and nonprofit leaders who focus on elder abuse policy, and the Elder Death Review Team at the West Tennessee Regional Forensic Center, which examines cases with suspicious circumstances for possible elder abuse.

All of these remarkable teams represent a united effort to protect older adults in Shelby County, a population that is steadily growing as baby boomers become seniors. That means the need for support services also will increase, as will the possibilities of abuse.

Older adults have a wealth of skills and knowledge they have developed over a lifetime of experiences. They add strength and wisdom to our community. Let's all work in any way we can to prevent elder abuse before it happens.

Tennessee state law requires reporting of suspected abuse of a vulnerable or elderly adult.

Tips When Hiring a Home Health Care Agency or Independent Caregiver

When hiring a caregiver, you often don't know whether you'll need the person for a week, a month or possibly years. Hiring the right qualified person is essential. You are needing someone to take care of your loved one so you need to do your homework. Treat this like a business because it is your personal business.

- ☐ Interview at least four agencies or independent caregivers. The more the better.

- ☐ Confirm the agency is Certified and Licensed in Home Health Care with the State Health Department.

- ☐ Tell them exactly what your needs are and how many hours a day you need.

- ☐ Ask the fee on the hours and days you need. The fee may vary depending on nights, weekends and holidays.

- ☐ What are the logistics for payment? Weekly or biweekly? Check, credit card, ACH?

- ☐ Can the agency/caregiver be flexible with you on the hours and days?

- ☐ Who will be your main contact? Is there another contact for "after hours"?

- ☐ Ask the agency for references.
- ☐ How long has the agency been in business?
- ☐ Will the agency cooperate with a Long Term Health Care Insurance Carrier?
- ☐ How does the agency screen the caregiver?
- ☐ Is there a background check? If so, when? Drug Test? If so, when?
- ☐ Ask to meet the agency caregivers before the first day at your home.
- ☐ Are the caregivers required to continue their education on quality home care?
- ☐ Do you need a Certified Nursing Assistant (CNA)? Most caregivers might not be a CNA.

When hiring an independent caregiver, do the interview at your loved one's home.
When you hire a caregiver, do a background check. Drug Screen?

Questions to ask during an interview with caregiver:

- ☐ Have they been fingerprinted?
- ☐ Individual Caregiver References Provided?
- ☐ What makes them want to do this kind of work?
- ☐ Recall a time a client tried your patience—how did you respond?
- ☐ How would they handle a stressful situation?
- ☐ Tell me a mistake you made with a client—What did you do to make it right?

Tips on Hiring and Brief Questionnaire

☐ Have they previously cared for an Alzheimer or Parkinson's person?

☐ Do they mind doing light housekeeping and cooking? What do they like to cook?

☐ If they are driving your loved one, do they have insurance?

☐ Whose insurance will cover them and the vehicle if there is an accident?

☐ Are they familiar with first aid, wound care, CPR?

☐ What personal care/hygiene tasks are needed? Are they comfortable doing them?

☐ Will they be encouraging to play some games to keep the brain active?

☐ If appropriate, will they encourage to socialize and not isolate?

☐ What is the agency or caregiver's Safety Guidelines? For example, when to wear masks/gloves/take temperature?

☐ How often will the Care Plan be evaluated and updated?

☐ What is the policy for communication? **Communication is Paramount!**

As you interview potential caregivers, consider the following:

Does the person seem respectful as well as empathetic?

Is the person talkative or quiet?

Does the person seem patient, reliable and observant of the surroundings?

You are in charge of the services that are provided. Pay regularly and pay fair wages.

You will need to provide a 1099 (independent contractor) statement at the end of the year.

Shop around and compare services and fees from the different agencies and individual caregivers. They may or may not be Certified Nursing Assistants (CNA's)

When you hire a capable and honest caregiver, treat the person well because you will want them to stay with your loved one for as long as possible.

Brief Estate Planning and Other Key Questions

Do you live by yourself? Yes _____ No _____

Do you have a life alert? _____

Why not? _____

Do you have a "Payable on Death" (POD) on your financial accounts? Yes_____ No _____

Why not? _____

Do you have a "Transfer on Death" (TOD) on your assets? Yes_____ No_____

Do you have a "Power of Attorney"? For Financial and Health? Yes _____ No _____

Why not? _____

Did you know that your designated Power of Attorney no longer has authority to make decisions once you're gone? All decisions regarding your estate are now in the hands of the Executor of your Trust/Estate. Often POA's are also Executors.

Do you have a "Do Not Resuscitate" (DNR)? Yes _____ No _____

Do you have a Living Will? Yes _____ No_____
It designates the person's wishes in the event they cannot speak for themselves as opposed to just saying Do Not Resuscitate.

Do you have a Trust? Yes _____ No _____

Why not? _____

Do you have a Will? Yes _____ No _____

Why not? _____

If you have assets of more than $50,000, and do not wish to assign POD's, you need to have a Trust. If you only have a Will, the State will most likely send to probate court which could take up to two years to settle in court, along with the court costs.

If you have prepared such documents, are they up to date with your attorney? Yes _____ No _____

When were they last updated? _____

Are there changes that need to be made? Yes _____ No _____

Do you meet yearly with your executor(s) to make sure they understand your wishes? _____

Does someone know where your financial/legal/medical documents are? Yes _____ No _____

Is your residence organized & decluttered? Yes _____ No _____

Have you gone through heirlooms, furniture, mementos and items of personal significance to designate who receives what? Have you marked each item with tape or a tag to name who should get this when you're gone?

What about electronics, lawn mower, tractor, tools, guns, jewelry? It is advised that you add to your Will a list of designated items with the names of who receives what. Sign and date this list to avoid any confusion. Some people meet individually with their children and grandchildren to ask them what they would like.

Have you stopped mail solicitations, catalogues, and unnecessary mailings? _____

Do not just throw them away, you must notify the sender to Cease Sending.

Have you determined who will take care of your pets?
Yes _____ No _____

Have you considered a retirement facility? Yes _____ No _____

Do you think you might consider one within the next 2 years?
Yes _____ No _____

If you answered Yes, do you have them written down and/or have you visited them?

What will you do when you can no longer drive?
_____

Do you have your utility bills and other regular bills on "Automatic Draft"? Yes _____ No_____

Gather your computer account passwords.
Gather or provide information to close your business.
Gather proper identification.
Identify Accounts that should be closed or merged.
Determine any debts that need to be made aware.
Do you have a list made of your funeral arrangements? What would you like?
Do not pre-purchase funeral arrangements, just let your loved one know your wishes.

Are you an organ donor? Yes_____ No_____

Do you have a pre-arranged funeral? (NOT prepaid)
Yes_____ No_____

Do you have a list of your friend's names and how they are meaningful to you?

   Perhaps you would like that shared with your family.

Have you educated yourself about Hospice? Hospice is for people who have been told by a doctor that they have less than 6 months to live. Most hospice care is done at home (90%). Hospice does not cover the cost of caregivers, but Hospice does provide a CNA to bathe the client twice a week, and nurses who are on-call 24/7 to check on the patient and keep the patient medically comfortable (these are usually one-hour visits). Hospice also provides social workers and chaplains. If a patient is on Medicare, all Hospice expenses, including medications and medical equipment, are covered. On occasion, they might provide a volunteer to alleviate the home caregiver.

~ * ~

If this book has given you some ideas and information to assist you in your venture of home health care, I would certainly appreciate a couple of minutes of your time to post a review.

RESOURCES

For a comprehensive list of websites related to topics throughout this book, go to:

        https://CareGiverScareTakers.com/

Made in the USA
Monee, IL
16 February 2022